Fine WoodWorking

on **Marquetry and Veneer**

Fine WoodWorking® *on* Marquetry and Veneer

38 articles selected by the editors of *Fine Woodworking* magazine

The Taunton Press

Cover photo by Paul Bertorelli

BOOKS & VIDEOS

for fellow enthusiasts

First printing: January 1987
Second printing: April 1988
Third printing: October 1990
Fourth printing: September 1994
Fifth printing: December 1996
International Standard Book Number: 0-918804-74-4
Library of Congress Catalog Card Number: 86-51291
Printed in the United States of America

A FINE WOODWORKING Book

FINE WOODWORKING® is a trademark of The Taunton Press, Inc.,
registered in the U.S. Patent and Trademark Office.

The Taunton Press, Inc.
63 South Main Street
Box 5506
Newtown, CT 06470-5506

Contents

Introduction

Perhaps it is just human nature, but the most beautiful pieces of wood seem always to come from the farthest, most inaccessible corners of the globe. Naturally such wood is scarce and expensive, and we must make each piece of it stretch as far as it can. Hence the craft of veneering, whereby we slice or saw beautiful woods into thin leaves, and glue this precious material onto a substructure of more common stuff.

The allied art of marquetry consists of making pictures, jigsaw-puzzle fashion, from a palette of colorful wood veneers. The world's most elegant furniture, made for the kings of Europe during the 18th century, typically featured marquetry panels set into veneered carcases.

In 38 articles reprinted from the first ten years of *Fine Woodworking* magazine, authors who are also craftsmen reveal the secrets of working with veneers. They explain how veneer is manufactured and how you can saw your own, how to lay it using simple equipment, and how to design furniture based on veneered panels. The methods of the marquetarian are also described in detail, with particular attention to shop-built saws for cutting the most intricate details. Finally, there's a discussion of working with that modern, man-made equivalent of veneer, plastic laminate.

John Kelsey, editor

Veneer

The commercial facts of life

by Lee S. Jacobs

The log opens, the sawyer smiles, the mill owner nods his approval and the log buyer sighs with relief. Whether the log is from a steaming jungle, a distant forest, a local wood or someone's front lawn, uncertainty exists until this crucial moment. If no interior defects develop in cutting and if the manufacturing technique is flawless, this log will produce fine veneer.

Only prime logs of each species are used for veneers. Trees large in diameter, tall, straight and healthy are sought. The challenge for veneer-mill operators is always to find the finest logs, anywhere in the world. Veneer logs command a premium that ranges from double or triple the value of lumber logs to many times this value, depending on the species and the circumstances in the market at the time of purchase.

The cost of veneer logs makes it important to extract the most from every one. Sawing these logs into lumber is extremely wasteful because each saw kerf might destroy the equivalent of five or six sheets of veneer—or even more. One board 12 inches wide and 10 feet long produces 10 board feet, or 10 square feet of lumber. But if it had been cut into veneer, there would have been 300 square feet, all beautifully matched.

Today, as in centuries past, veneer men seek the beauty, warmth and versatility found only in hardwoods, the deciduous or broad-leaved trees that are the prime source of outstanding wood. Out of 90,000 known varieties of hardwood, no more than 200 are available in commercial quantities. At any one time perhaps 50 species are in vogue in North America. In the mid-1970's, plain white oak, plain red oak, pecan, walnut and knotty pine were most popular. In the previous twenty years, walnut, cherry, mahogany, pecan and oak (in that order) were the prominent species. Demand for a species depends on the design: French provincial usually suggests cherry; colonial furniture demands maple, birch or knotty pine; traditional generally requires mahogany or walnut; modern design might use rosewood or teak. Designers and manufacturers constantly search for something new and interesting and as a consequence the popularity of various species constantly changes.

Veneering dates back to 2000 B. C. Veneer was prized through the Egyptian, Greek and Roman eras. During the 18th and 19th centuries, the furniture masters used veneer extensively, although their veneered furniture was available to only a select few. Originally, users of veneer sawed wood into thin sheets by hand to obtain more of a particular grain pattern and to gain more control of the wood. These sheets were then applied to a thick piece of wood, using animal glue and hot sandbags for heat and pressure, to become an outer layer or face.

Veneering has developed into a refined art and modern veneer mills are geared to serve the furniture and construction businesses, much as steel mills serve the automobile industry. The veneer industry developed parallel to the development of glues—the synthetic resin glues of the 1930's and 40's which revolutionized panel making.

Veneer is made, bought and sold by the flitch. This term applies both to the uncut segment of a log and to the stack of veneers cut from it. A flitch can be half a log, a quarter or a sixth, depending on the size of the tree. A mahogany tree, for example, might consist of three or four large logs. Each log might be sawed into six flitches. Such a giant tree of 18 to 24 flitches could yield 80,000 to 90,000 square feet of veneer. Generally a tree yields one veneer log which would be divided into two or perhaps four flitches. The yield would vary from several thousand square feet to a maximum of ten thousand, depending on the log size. Walnut logs usually produce two flitches of 1,500 to 3,500 square feet each.

There are three basic ways of cutting veneers: sawing, slicing and rotary peeling. Sawing, the oldest method, is rarely done today. It is slow, wasteful and cumbersome. Still, saws can produce veneer in longer pieces than a slicer or rotary veneer lathe can make. Saws are also used to cut heavy thicknesses of dense woods that would put undue strain on slicers or lathes during extended production. But veneer saws produce a thick kerf, and not only is valuable wood lost as sawdust but also a close match of veneers is impossible. Veneer sawing is extremely slow compared to the high speeds of slicers and rotary lathes. Yet in certain very specialized uses, sawed veneer is preferred for it is claimed that this process less severely ruptures the wood fibers.

The vertical slicer is a modern engineering masterpiece. Developed in the early 1900's, the oldest slicer is as modern as the newest, due to the genius of its inventor. Every improvement since its inception is only an adaptation of the basic slicer. Face woods for cabinetry—commonly walnut, cherry, oak, mahogany, teak and rosewood—are sliced. The flitch is cleaned and then mounted almost horizontally between dogs on the slicer bed. The machine swings the entire flitch up and down against a horizontal knife, which moves incrementally inward as each slice is sheared away. The sight and sound of a thousand pounds of wood hitting a razor-sharp knife at a rate of 60 to 90 times a minute is impressive indeed.

The vertical slicer makes no kerf and thus the leaves are almost perfectly matched. It can cut veneers from 1/120 to

From *Fine Woodworking* magazine (Fall 1976) 4:33-34

3/32 inch in thickness and up to 225 inches long. It is critical to keep the veneers assembled in the order they come from the flitch, one sheet on top of another, in order to book match, slip match and accomplish all the ingenious patterns of veneering.

The thinner the veneer, the more accurate the match, but the more fragile. The limit of practical thinness is the skill of the panel-maker. Veneer 1/85 inch or thinner is difficult to joint, splice, fabricate, sand and finish. Consequently most veneer is cut to 1/30 inch, which presents practically no trouble. Other thicknesses, particularly 1/20, 1/16 and 1/8 inch, are used in limited quantities for special purposes such as edge banding table and desk tops.

Horizontal slicers are used in various parts of the world to cut both face and core woods. On these machines the wood is stationary, mounted in a pit, and a knife is drawn across the wood horizontally. Generally this process is slower and more costly, though it has advantages in cutting wide flitches.

The interior and back components of a veneered panel are cut on a true rotary lathe. These machines are generally 36 to 150 inches long and can swing logs up to 78 inches in diameter. A log is chucked at both ends and the veneer unwinds like a roll of paper. Veneers thus peeled from logs of poplar, gum, basswood and many tropical woods are inexpensive, relatively stable and easy to cut. The usual thickness is 1/24 inch for crossbanding and backs. Heavier thicknesses are also cut to build up veneered panels. Rotary-cut woods are generally nondescript, used to impart strength and balance to panels. Birch, maple, red oak, elm and mahogany are rotary-cut to produce a less expensive face for stock panel and door production.

A variation of rotary cutting is known as "half-rounding." Face woods produced by this method are similar in appearance to sliced woods. A flitch is prepared in the same manner as for slicing, attached to a metal stay-log and rotated against the knife. The veneer produced by each revolution of the lathe is between the classic sliced or true cathedral figure made by a slicer, and the undulating figure of the rotary lathe. In a single species, flitches half-rounded will yield wider widths and wilder grain patterns than sliced flitches.

Softwood veneers for the construction plywood industry are always cut on a rotary lathe. The hardwood and softwood industries are different from each other in almost every aspect, from logging to final use. With the one exception of hardwood faces on pine and fir cores, the two industries have very little in common.

Veneer is sold by resident representatives of veneer mills located in furniture manufacturing centers. The mills usually have sample rooms for the convenience of large veneer buyers, architects and designers. Samples of veneer are also taken to woodworking plants for selection.

Large furniture plants require a truckload or more of veneer per day. Veneer buying for such a plant is a full-time job, the buyer inspecting millions of feet of veneer daily. Generally, veneer is purchased for "cutting of a suite" and the amount bought depends on the number of suites in a cutting. A large factory might, for example, plan a run of 500 bedroom suites—bed, bureau and dressing table—and the buyer would have to amass enough veneer, perhaps from a number of mills, to do the entire job. Thus the amount of veneer he would purchase might range from a truckload up to 250,000 feet or even more, depending on the price range of the

furniture, the plant size, the method of construction and the current market. Smaller plants usually designate one person a veneer buyer, most often the plant owner, plant manager, veneer-room foreman or purchasing agent. The job is always considered very responsible because of the large amount of money involved and the judgment required to buy the exact veneer necessary for the furniture to be made.

The modern veneer industry started in the early 1900's. Face mills were located primarily in the Midwest, in Indiana and Kentucky where oak and walnut were plentiful. There were coastal mills located at major ports in New Jersey and Virginia to cut imported woods. Today, there are more than 40 face veneer mills and almost 200 rotary mills. Rotary mills are found from the Gulf of Mexico to northern Canada and from the Atlantic Ocean to the Mississippi River. Most veneer mills are small and many are still family-owned. A small operation cutting 40 million to 150 million feet per year seems to be optimum. Such a mill might, in a single day, ship 15 to 20 truckloads, each of 250,000 square feet of veneer, into the giant furniture center in the Carolinas, called the "Furniture South." Other furniture centers, using considerably smaller quantities, are located in Grand Rapids, Memphis, Los Angeles and eastern Canada. Face veneer industry produces five to ten billion feet of veneer per year. Rotary mills produce 20 billion feet, although the amount of rotary-cut wood used for crossbanding has decreased in recent years due to increased use of particleboard. Imported veneers, both face and center stock, might total another three to five billion feet a year in North America.

The export demand for veneer logs keeps the market in a constant state of flux. Domestic mills generally buy veneer logs along with saw logs, but export buyers buy only veneer logs and are able to pay top dollar for them. And, since European mills usually slice the veneer thinner than American mills do, a given log of top quality is worth more in Europe. When walnut was hot several years ago, European mills would go up to $7 a board foot. As a result, good-quality logs became quite scarce. Then the fashion overseas changed, and the price in the mid-1970's was down to $1 or $2. The supply hadn't really changed, though, and when the export price drops that way, the domestic market usually starts buying.

Domestic mills have only recently become aware of the huge export market; they now cut veneer for export as well as for U. S. production. The Japanese furniture industry in particular has an enormous effect on the world market, because it is very large and has no domestic forests to exploit. Complicating matters is the recent trend among Third World countries to follow the lead of the oil producers and embargo log exports, forcing the price up.

Against all this, the craftsman may require 100 or 200 square feet of veneer for one commissioned piece of furniture. Fortunately for him, there are veneer merchants who specialize in small quantities of high-quality woods. Such companies generally buy unusual and outstanding flitches, the best available, directly from the mills. They are willing to sell one flitch or to break a flitch and sell books of several sheets.

The veneer industry, having as its basic raw material one of nature's true marvels—trees—is a healthy, growing industry. For as long as trees continue to grow and renew themselves, the cutters of veneer will search the world for logs to find the beauty, warmth and variety that nature has concealed. □

Knife Checks in Veneer

How they are formed, how to cope with them

by R. Bruce Hoadley

When considering veneer and its quality, we usually think only of characteristics such as species, thickness and figure, or defects such as knots, stain or pitch streaks. Beyond that, veneer is veneer. But of most serious concern should be knife checks. These are parallel-to-grain fracture planes produced in the veneer at the time of its manufacture and which may go unnoticed, only to cause agonizing problems later. Because they are probably the most common cause of checks in the finished surfaces of veneered work, the woodworker should understand what these knife checks are, how they are formed, how to detect them and how to cope with them.

Sawn veneer does not have these checks, but today most veneer is knife-cut by peeling (rotary cutting) or slicing. In either method, the basic cutting action is similar. A knife sharpened to an angle approaching 0° would distort the wood structure the least, but would, of course, break too easily. Veneer-cutting knives are therefore sharpened to an angle of about 21°—a compromise between a small angle that would minimize distortion of the wood structure and a blunt angle that would minimize knife breakage. This means that as the knife separates the veneer from the flitch, the separated layer of wood is severely bent, and stresses build up in the region near the knife edge. When the strength of the wood is exceeded, the stress is relieved by failure, and the plane of failure thus formed is called a knife check, or lathe check. This bending and breaking cycle is repeated as cutting continues, so each layer of veneer has checks at fairly regular intervals.

The side of the veneer that was against the knife and has knife checks penetrating into its surface is called the loose side, or open face. The other side is called the tight side, or closed face.

To prevent knife checks, lathes and slicers are equipped with a pressure bar or nosebar, a solid bar or roller that bears against the veneer as it is being cut. Its pressure holds the cell structure together in the region where checks usually develop. Too much pressure crushes the cell structure of the veneer, so there is a theoretical optimum opening between the knife and the pressure bar that produces the highest-quality veneer. Experience has shown that checks can be minimized or eliminated when the distance between the pressure bar and the knife is 80% to 90% of the thickness of the cut.

The terms tightness and looseness refer to the relative depth of knife checks. In producing veneer without nosebar pressure, tightness is improved by cutting lower-density species of wood, by heating the wood, and by thin cuts.

Anatomical features of the species being cut are also related to checking. If structural planes of weakness—such as the large rays of oak or the earlywood layer in ring-porous hardwoods—coincide with the probable plane of check formation, the checks will be worse. Diffuse-porous hardwoods with fine, well-distributed rays are more likely to yield tight, uniform veneer.

The tightness of veneer can be assessed in a number of ways. Surface roughness or corrugation (especially of the loose side) is commonly associated with checking. Veneer having any suggestion of a washboard surface is probably loosely cut.

Manually flexing the veneer will help you see the checks. In addition, the veneer will feel stiffer when flexed to close the checks, but will feel more limp when the checks are flexed open. Tightly cut veneer will flex about as easily both ways, so if you can't tell, it's probably cut well.

In some woodworking applications, it is critical to know the

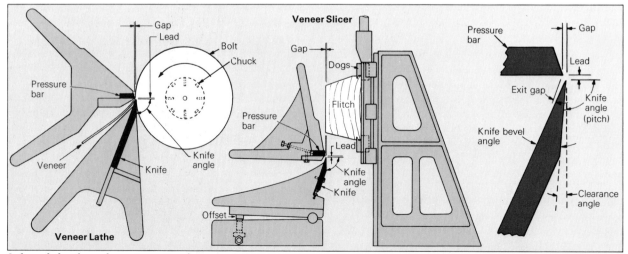

Softwoods for plywood are rotary-cut with a veneer lathe, left, while hardwood veneers are usually sliced, center. The diagram at right shows the relationships between pressure bar and knife, which determine the quality of the veneer.

From *Fine Woodworking* magazine (September 1978) 12:83-85

With nosebar retracted, left, veneer checks seriously as it curls over the knife. A little nosebar pressure, center, reduces the amount of checking. When the nosebar pressure approaches 15% to 20% of the veneer thickness, right, checks are nearly eliminated.

actual depth of the checks. This can be determined by staining with an alcohol or spirit solution of dye such as machinists' layout dye, then beveling the veneer. Cut sample strips of veneer from the ends of sheets and stain them liberally on both sides, keeping the stain away from end grain. Allow to dry thoroughly, then glue or cement the veneer onto blocks of scrap wood. When the glue is set, bevel the veneer with a fine sander disc, or with a sharp chisel or knife. The relative depth of the checks will be apparent across the bevel.

The consequences of knife checks should be quite obvious. The most common problem is parallel-to-grain cracks in the finish on veneered surfaces—nearly always traceable to knife checks. This problem is especially aggravating because it is usually a delayed reaction, appearing months or years after the piece is finished. A surface may be flawless at completion, but the normal shrinking and swelling of the wood in response to seasonal humidity fluctuation cause hidden knife checks to migrate to the surface and through the finish itself.

This problem is second only to delamination as a cause of the bad reputation veneered products have undeservedly acquired. One frequently sees it when softwood structural plywood such as Douglas fir is used for finished or painted surfaces. Structural plywood is designed to carry stresses parallel to the grain direction of its plies, and this capability is little affected by knife checks. Apparently, little serious effort is made to control tightness of veneer in manufacturing commercial softwood plywood. Plywood manufactured with surfaces of medium or high-density impregnated paper overlay (designated M.D.O. and H.D.O.) is best where smooth painted surfaces are needed. Large lumberyards usually stock M.D.O. plywood, which is routinely used for outdoor signs and similar products.

End-grain plywood surfaces may also reveal finish defects caused by knife checks. This is especially common when moisture loss results in excessive shrinkage stress.

Another visual effect of knife checks is bleed-through of glue, which shows up as a series of evenly spaced lines on the veneered surface. This is especially apparent in light-colored woods such as maple or birch sapwood.

In woodworking, veneer should routinely be inspected for tightness. Checks penetrating no more than 25% of the thickness of the veneer can be tolerated under most circumstances. When laying up veneer, spread the loose side with glue. With luck, the glue will penetrate the checks and perhaps glue them closed. It may help to lay the veneer over a slightly convex surface so the checks will be open to the glue. (This will also ensure that the tight side is the exposed face on surface plies.) Care must then be taken not to sand through the tight side of the veneer. I have seen countless situations where veneer surfaces have been sanded right down to expose the knife checks—and the glue in them.

Bookmatched surfaces are a predicament, because the veneers must be placed with alternate open and closed faces up. In such cases, it is important to have relatively tight veneer to ensure uniformity. You may have seen bookmatched patterns in which the finish quality alternated with each piece of veneer, a consequence of knife checks.

Lathe-check troubles are not limited to visual surface effects. Critical mechanical problems may also result. Most typical is some form of rolling shear developed when plywood is stressed in the form of a beam over a short span, so that high

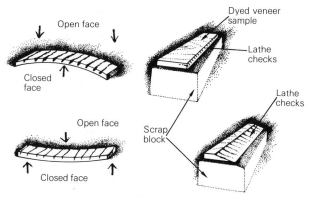

Loosely cut veneer feels more limp when the checks are flexed open, stiffer when the checks are closed. To gauge check depth, dye both sides of a sample and glue it to scrap wood. Bevel the veneer and compare the dye penetration to the bevel length.

This maple veneer is so loose that the surface is corrugated.

Core veneers in fir plywood are usually checked.

Left, checks broke through paint on fir plywood in a year. Baltic-birch panel, right, was smooth when finished with Deft two years ago.

levels of horizontal shear are developed. If the shear coincides with the direction of stress that opens the checks, rolling shear failure may result. The edges of plywood panels "broomed" over in this manner are often misinterpreted as "delamination," which erroneously implies glue failure.

I do not have any specific recommendations for finishing veneer that has knife checks. I think a finish that would provide the best moisture barrier and thus reduce dimensional variation would be best. Also, if the checks were on the surface, any finish that would seal them shut would help. A fin-

Bruce Hoadley is professor of wood science and technology at the University of Massachusetts, Amherst. He wrote his doctoral dissertation on veneer cutting.

ish like linseed oil would have little to offer. A low-viscosity lacquer or varnish in multiple coats might work best.

On the whole, most hardwood cabinet veneer produced by reputable mills is cut with adequate production quality control to ensure reasonable tightness. But beware of "clearance" sales or "closeouts," because loose veneer is hardly a bargain at any price. The best guideline is to buy veneer from reputable dealers and know how to detect, and cope with, the occasional loose veneer. □

EDITOR'S NOTE: Impregnated paper overlay for plywood is available in roll form, usually in 52-in. widths. It has no grain direction and is often glued down as crossbanding when veneering over plywood or chipboard. One brand is "Yorkite," manufactured by NVF Co. of Yorkland, Del.

This simple cutting experiment will help you understand how knife checks develop and affect veneer.

1 *Crosscut four to six 1-in. sections from the end of a plank of medium or low-density wood with even grain (e.g., eastern white pine, basswood).*

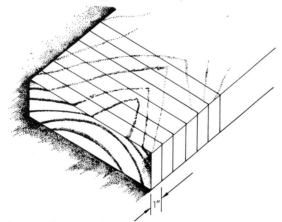

2 *Immerse the wood in water for several days. (The idea is to bring the wood back to the fiber-saturation point. If you start with green wood, the soaking is unnecessary.)*

3 *When ready to cut, heat half the pieces to near boiling while still immersed. Allow at least an hour for the pieces to heat through.*

4 *Clamp a cold piece in a wood vise, side grain up.*

5 *Using a block plane with the throat opened up and the iron set for a thick cut ($\frac{1}{16}$ in.), plane across the grain a ribbon of wood from the 1-in. face. Your "shaving" will be a strip of veneer.*

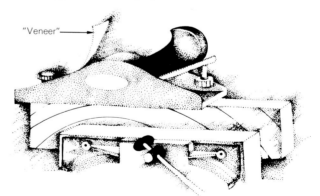

"Veneer"—

In cutting, you will probably feel the regular clickety feeling of the cyclic knife checking. Since your plane does not have a nosebar, your "veneer" will probably have lots of knife checks. Experiment with different thicknesses of cut and with the hot pieces. Notice how much tighter the veneer is when you cut it thinner. Or when hot wood is cut. Can you readily recognize the "open" and "closed" faces in every strip?

Bandsaw Your Own Veneer

All it takes is patience and a sharp blade

by Brad Walters and Richard Barsky

Anyone who has worked with commercially cut veneer knows that it can be tricky stuff to handle. Because it's so thin, sliced veneer doesn't gracefully suffer the dings and dents of hard use, and the margin for error—especially where two veneered panels adjoin—is quite small. One alternative worth trying is bandsawing your own thick veneer, a method that has several advantages over buying thinner stuff. Prepared veneers usually come in thicknesses between $\frac{1}{28}$ in. and $\frac{1}{32}$ in., but when you saw your own, you decide the thickness. In our shop, we usually aim for a $\frac{1}{8}$-in. finished thickness.

Because sawn veneers are thicker, they work and feel more like solid wood, yet still retain the stability of veneer. Gluing the veneer to the substrate is easier, too—none of that curling, bubbling, splitting and the like to contend with. You'll also have more material to scrape, plane and sand when flushing up adjacent surfaces, so you won't have to worry about going through the face veneer and exposing the substrate.

Sawn veneers are cut by resawing (standing a board on its edge and bandsawing through its thickness), in this case into a number of thin slices. To resaw veneer, you'll need a bandsaw of adequate size and power. We use an old 26-in. cast-iron Silver bandsaw with a 5-HP motor. With a sharp 1-in. wide blade, it will handle anything we feed it, up to its $10\frac{3}{4}$-in. depth of cut. While a big bandsaw makes this job easier, don't be discouraged if you own a smaller machine. All bandsaws have limitations, but if you work at it, you might discover that your little saw will do just fine with narrower boards. Experimentation is the rule; try some scraps to find out just how wide your saw can go.

Before doing any cutting, check over your saw—there are some things you can do to improve its performance. The drive belt(s) should be tight and in good condition. The blade must be sharp and well-tensioned ($\frac{1}{4}$ in. of flex with light finger pressure is good), and it should track smoothly. Make sure the bandsaw's tires are in good shape, and if they are glossed over with pitch from sawing softwoods, remove the blade and clean the rubber with lacquer thinner. Adjust ball-bearing thrust guides so they barely touch the back of the blade as it's running with no cutting load. Set fiber (or steel) guide blocks to bear lightly on the blade just behind the bottom of each tooth's gullet.

For resawing, we've found that a wide blade with a lot of set works best. We use a 1-in. skiptooth blade with four teeth per inch. If your machine won't accommodate this width, you can use a narrower blade; the wider the better, though, as the stiffness of the wider band makes for straighter cuts. Go ahead and experiment with other tooth patterns and sizes, but keep in mind that a coarse blade will cut more aggressively and may take a

With a sharp blade, well-adjusted guides and a stout fence, any bandsaw can cut veneers. Guided by a shopmade single-point fence, the authors' 26-in., 5-HP machine will saw boards up to 10¾ in. wide.

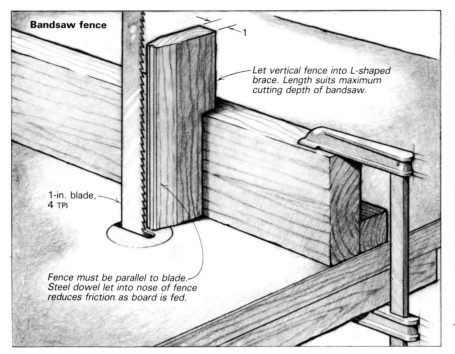

Bandsaw fence

1

Let vertical fence into L-shaped brace. Length suits maximum cutting depth of bandsaw.

1-in. blade, 4 TPI

Fence must be parallel to blade. Steel dowel let into nose of fence reduces friction as board is fed.

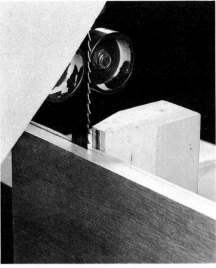

With the trailing edge of the fence positioned ⅛ in. in front of the blade, begin the cut by pressing the board against the fence just ahead of the blade. Follow the marking-gauge line (pencil-darkened for clarity) by pivoting the board on the fence.

wider kerf. A finer blade will yield a smoother if slower cut, but it will dull more quickly.

Once your bandsaw is ready, you need a fence to steady the wood so you can resaw veneer of uniform thickness. There are two kinds of fences: single-point and straight. We use the single-point, but each type has its own merits and drawbacks. As the drawing above shows, our single-point fence consists of a 10¾-in. high vertical member attached to an L-shaped brace that we clamp to the saw's table. Where the fence's pointed nose bears against the stock, we epoxied a ⅛-in. steel dowel into a groove, which reduces friction as the board is fed. This allows the stock to be "steered" as it's cut, which is helpful because the angle of feed can change slightly as the blade gets duller, and with variations in the hardness of the wood. Also, even a sharp blade will often have "lead," a condition where the teeth on one side of the blade are sharper than those on the other side, causing the cut to drift off toward the sharper side. You'll need to adjust the feed angle to compensate.

The straight fence is similar to a tablesaw rip fence, and because it supports the board along its length as well as across its width, cutting can proceed more quickly—if your stock is flat and straight. If the board is at all irregular, you won't have room to steer it to make corrections as the cut proceeds. Also, you can't make the steering adjustments for blade lead.

Before you set up the fence, decide what thickness to cut your veneer. This will vary, depending on the board you begin with and how many veneers you want out of it. We usually plan on one veneer leaf per ¼ in. of original thickness. This is generous and may seem wasteful, but it assures us of getting finished leaves of ³⁄₃₂-in. to ⅛-in. thickness. If we want more mileage out of a board, we may try for more leaves—four out of a ¾-in. board, for instance. With smooth, straight cuts we can still get a good finished thickness, but with bowed, warped or wide lumber this is risky. Experience will teach you the limitations.

Rather than set your fence for a standard thickness, look at your board and decide how many veneers you want from it, then divide the thickness into that many sections. Since the saw takes

a kerf each time you slice off a veneer, you have to account for this loss in your figuring. Multiply the kerf size times the number of cuts (one less than the number of veneers you want) and subtract that from the total thickness. Divide the remainder by the number of veneers you're going for, and you'll arrive at the actual thickness of each leaf. For instance, if we had a ¹⁵⁄₁₆-in. board and decided to get four veneers out of it, it would take three cuts to do it. Our saw takes a ¹⁄₁₆-in. kerf, so the total loss would be ³⁄₁₆ in., leaving ¹²⁄₁₆ in. to divide between the four veneers, or ³⁄₁₆ in. per veneer. If this is cutting it too close, you can go for one less veneer so you'll be less likely to wind up with a useless cutoff.

To set up, position the single-point fence so that the board contacts the fence about ⅛ in. before the cut begins. Use a steel rule to measure from the fence to the *inside* (closest to the fence) set of the blade, and measure from the top and the bottom of the fence to be sure it's parallel to the blade. This is important and should be accurate to within ¹⁄₆₄ in., otherwise you will cut wedges. Clamp both ends of the fence securely and check the measurement again. Usually you will need to loosen the clamps and make slight adjustments, or, if your saw has one, adjust the tilting table. If all else fails, place a small shim where the fence meets the bandsaw table to bring it parallel to the blade. Simply shifting the position of the clamp may also do it.

To prepare your board for sawing, surface it so the faces are flat, then joint and rip both edges square to the face and parallel to each other. If you plan to bookmatch, leave the length generous (especially if the grain is a cathedral pattern) because you'll often have to shift the veneers quite a bit to get them to line up. To give yourself an accurate reference for measuring the cut's progress, scribe a line along the top edge of the board with a marking gauge set to the thickness of cut. Also mark the butt end of each board with a bold V as a reference mark for matching later on. Now you're ready to go.

In sawing veneers, it's important to hold the face of the board firmly against the fence at the cutting point. You do this by pressing on the outside face of the board, just in front of the blade. Feed with one hand, and apply a steady but gentle pressure with

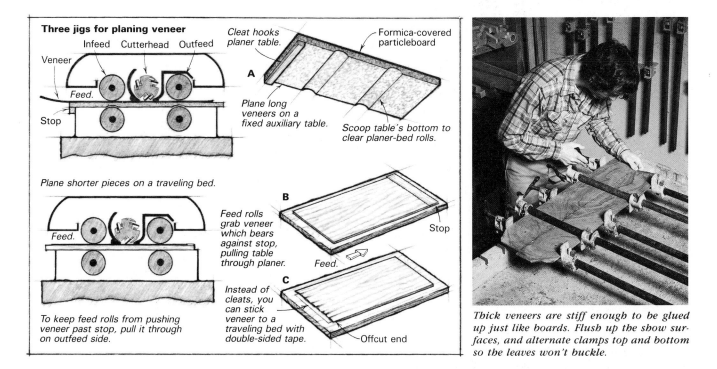

Three jigs for planing veneer

Infeed Cutterhead Outfeed

Veneer

Feed.

Stop

Plane shorter pieces on a traveling bed.

Feed.

To keep feed rolls from pushing veneer past stop, pull it through on outfeed side.

Cleat hooks planer table.

Formica-covered particleboard

A

Plane long veneers on a fixed auxiliary table.

Scoop table's bottom to clear planer-bed rolls.

B

Feed rolls grab veneer which bears against stop, pulling table through planer.

Stop

Feed.

C

Instead of cleats, you can stick veneer to a traveling bed with double-sided tape.

Offcut end

Thick veneers are stiff enough to be glued up just like boards. Flush up the show surfaces, and alternate clamps top and bottom so the leaves won't buckle.

the other. As you saw, make sure you maintain this contact, but focus most of your attention on the top edge of the board, where the blade should be cutting just outside your scribed line. Go slowly at first. If the cut wanders, make gentle steering corrections. It's better to drift over the line a little and correct gradually than to over-correct larger wanderings. Once you've established a good cut, feed the board steadily, using a push stick to finish. The key is concentration, and with practice, it's not difficult.

If your first cut is good, mark another line on the top edge and make the second cut with the bandsawn surface against the fence. You'll get the most mileage out of your board and the best grain matchup if you resist the urge to resurface between cuts. If you are taking just three veneers out of a board, make the first cut, then flip the board and make the second with the other surfaced face against the fence.

Don't be discouraged if things go badly at first. It takes practice to get the hang of it. Here are a couple of pitfalls to watch out for. If you have to force the board, the blade is probably dull. If you push hard enough, the blade can heat up and twist as it passes through the wood, and may exit the board's face—which is a good reason to always keep your pressure hand in front of the blade. Also, the blade is liable to break under such stress. It's not worth ruining your composure and your veneer by trying to squeeze a little more life out of a blade. Save yourself time and grief by changing it. If your saw bogs down with a new blade, it may be underpowered. Try reducing the width of stock you're resawing, or switch to a coarser blade. Aside from a lack of experience, inaccuracies in the cut will likely be due to your setup. Shut the machine off and try to analyze what is happening. Patience and precision will pay off.

After the cutting is done, you have the pleasure of working with what James Krenov calls "real veneer." If you've gotten smooth, true cuts, you can use the veneer as is, gluing the bandsawn surface to your ground material, then sanding, planing or scraping the top. We find it worthwhile, however, to take our veneers to a neighboring shop where they are passed through a wide-belt abrasive planer. Local millwork or cabinet shops some-

times have these machines and will usually rent time on them. You can expect to lose about $\frac{1}{16}$ in. to the sander, depending on the regularity of your bandsaw cut. Using an auxiliary feed table as shown in the drawing, you may be able to pass veneers through a thickness planer. But be very careful, particularly with figured wood. It's dismaying to see a beautifully figured veneer come out of the planer in pieces.

When we're assembling veneers into larger panels, we do so before taking them to the sander. That way we have a fully prepared, flat panel ready for pressing as one sheet. Veneers at least $\frac{1}{8}$ in. thick are thick enough to be jointed and edge-glued just like regular boards. Alternate the clamps top and bottom and use light pressure—just enough to squeeze out a tiny bead of glue. Concentrate on flushing up the show face so irregularities in thickness will be on the back side—usually the sander will flatten them out. One word of caution here: Veneers sawn from thick boards may be relatively moist. To keep them from cracking later, give them a couple of days to reach equilibrium moisture content.

We won't go into the particulars of pressing here. For that, see Ian Kirby's article on pages 14-18. In veneering the back side of a panel, which you should do for stability, you have a couple of options. The best procedure is to cut additional veneers of the same species (although not of face quality) and of the same thickness. We've gotten good results, though, by using commercial veneers on the back side—usually mahogany veneer, which is available in wide pieces and is reasonably priced. We haven't had problems with the veneers being of different thicknesses.

Once resawing is added to your repertoire of skills, you'll find other uses for it. The technique will allow you to cut book-matched panels for frame-and-panel work, or to get two matched $\frac{3}{4}$-in. boards or three $\frac{1}{2}$-in. solid-wood drawer sides out of an 8/4 board. Essentially, you need no longer be restricted to the milled thicknesses available at the lumberyard. □

Brad Walters and Richard Barsky operate Dovetail Woodworks in Boulder, Colo.

Veneering
Preparing substrates is the first step

by Ian J. Kirby

Polished veneers: apple (top), padauk, maple burl, curly koa.

Veneering can lead to furniture designs that just aren't possible with solid wood. Lots of furniture has the shape it does because of wood's hygroscopic nature—you have to allow wood to expand and contract. Once you master veneering, however, you don't have that restriction. You can turn particleboard and fiberboard into dimensionally stable panels that are as attractive as any piece of solid wood, opening up a whole new world of design possibilities.

A veneer is simply a thin layer of wood, which can be glued on top of another material. At its best, veneering produces superb results. Done badly, it's a mess. You must plan every step before you begin. Unlike other woodworking, you don't start with a large plank and carve it down; you begin with a small piece and build it up to the size you want.

Veneering allows you to use woods that would be too expensive (rosewood or ebony) or just too unstable (burls or crotches) to be worked in solid form. Veneers have been available for centuries, of course, but what has now brought veneer into the small-shop woodworker's province is the advent of man-made substrates, the material onto which the veneer is glued. Particleboard and medium-density fiberboard have changed the whole nature of veneering.

In this article I'll discuss veneers (p. 13), and substrates and how to prepare them for veneering. Later articles deal with the application of veneers (pp. 14-18) and with design considerations when using veneered boards (pp. 20-24).

     •   •   •

Until the turn of this century, woodworkers had to make their own solid-wood substrates for veneering, and that was a real problem. If you veneer solid wood, laying the grain of the veneer at right angles to the grain of the solid wood, the veneer will come under tremendous stress as the substrate shrinks and expands, and can crack or delaminate. Even if you orient the grain of both materials in the same direction, you'll just have ordinary wood with a different wood glued onto it—with all of solid wood's moisture-related problems.

The traditional solution was to make large panels out of many small panels within frames, the assumption being that each little panel would shrink and expand less than one large panel would. It seems to have solved the problem in many cases, yet it shouldn't. Lots of little bits of wood will expand and contract collectively as much as one big piece of wood.

Today you can sidestep all of these problems by using particleboard or fiberboard as the substrate. These materials are so stable that seasonal movement is negligible. Probably the best substrate is medium-density fiberboard (MDF). It is made by breaking down wood into its fibrous form, then pressing the fibers back together again with an adhesive. All

MDF is basically the same: it has no grain, is square-edged and uniform throughout, and weighs about 48 lb. per cubic foot. It's a material that is very stable, but so boring that it cries out for the application of something with a little more life. Veneering both sides of a ⅝-in. thick MDF board produces a board thick enough for most furniture designs. You may have trouble finding MDF, since it is made primarily for industrial use. Some large lumber companies do carry it, although they may require a substantial minimum order. Professional woodworkers in your area may be able to recommend a local source of supply. Allied Plywood Corp. (which has seven warehouses along the East Coast) and Paxton Lumber Co. (which is headquartered in Kansas City, Mo., but has warehouses in several states) handle both MDF and furniture-quality particleboard. These materials are also available through some Georgia-Pacific Corp. service centers.

Plywood isn't a good substrate for veneering. Since it's made by gluing together layers of wood at right angles to each other, it has decent dimensional stability, but it can warp and twist. Particleboard, which is made by gluing wood particles together, is dimensionally stable, but some people get into an awful mess because they veneer onto building boards, not furniture-quality boards, which are multilayered boards with very smooth surfaces. Surface irregularities of the coarser building boards are liable to telegraph through the veneer. You can recognize furniture-quality boards (sometimes called industrial-grade) because they are oversize—a 4x8 sheet really measures 4 ft. 1 in. by 8 ft. 1 in. Building board is always 4x8, because builders commonly work to a 16-in. module.

The edges of man-made boards are just as boring as their surfaces. If the edges are going to show, you have to cover them in some way, as shown in figure 1. The usual technique is to glue a lipping of solid wood or veneer onto the edge of the substrate, clean it off, and glue veneer on both surfaces of the entire panel, including the lipping. Veneering the edges has one disadvantage: the edges will remain square after they're veneered. The only thing you can do to improve the ap-

From *Fine Woodworking* magazine (May 1984) 46:36-39

pearance and to help prevent chipping is to soften the veneered edges with sandpaper. You could make a softer edge by applying two or three layers of veneer so that you'd have more material to radius. One of the nice things you can do with veneer lipping, however, is to accent the edge treatment. If you wanted a five-veneer lipping, you could glue on three layers of the surface veneer and two layers of a different color veneer. This colored border picks out the edge and gives the job a lot of life.

For more shape on the edges, or what in woodworking terms is called molding, use solid-wood lipping. Other edge treatments include gluing on strips of leather, Naugahyde or even metal, such as fine copper foil.

In any case, decide what the lipping's width will be before you cut your substrate to size. The procedure is to first determine the size of the finished veneered panel, including the lipping. Then determine the width of the edge treatment, and subtract twice that from the length and width of the finished panel to get the dimensions of the substrate.

I prefer to glue the solid-wood lipping around the edge of the substrate before it's veneered. This gives enough material to mold the edges, and the surface veneer blends into the lipping, making the whole piece seem more cohesive. It's common to make the lipping of the same material as the surface veneer, but don't sacrifice a rare, exotic hardwood like ebony for lippings. Use a multilayer veneer lipping instead.

Lippings can be either mitered or butt-jointed at the corners, depending on the quality of the piece and the effect you want. With thin lippings, you can just about eliminate the visual effect of the butt joint by radiusing the corner. If you wish to miter the lipping, it's best to miter the lippings for the long edges before gluing them to the panel. If you do it this way, the lipping must be glued on very accurately, with no slippage along its length. On the short edges, when you're filling in, you have to cut the miter correctly at each end, and the length must be dead-accurate. Alternatively, you can glue the lipping on first and then cut the miters, but then you've got only one shot at getting them right.

The most common fault in making lippings is to have them too wide. The lipping should be the width needed to accommodate the molding on the edge, plus a safety margin of no more than $\frac{1}{8}$ in. So, if you want a $\frac{3}{4}$-in. thick edge rounded to a semicircle, all you need for lipping is $\frac{3}{8}$ in. plus a little, since $\frac{3}{8}$ in. is the radius of a $\frac{3}{4}$-in. circle.

The main reason for keeping lippings as narrow as possible is the shrinkage differential between the stable man-made substrate and the solid-wood lipping. After a few months, a wide lipping may shrink and show through the veneer, a condition known as telegraphing. Cost is also a consideration—you'd be surprised how much material goes into the lipping.

The simplest way to apply lipping is to keep the wood for the lipping wider than necessary until after it's glued onto the substrate. It will serve as its own clamping block, so you don't need a lot of clamps and battens, as you would if you

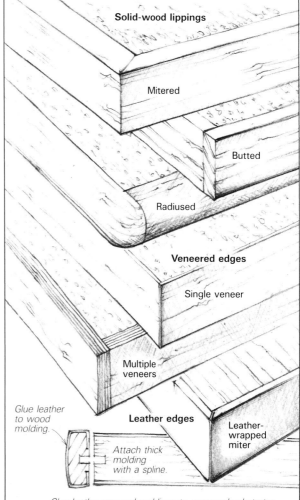

Fig. 1: Edge treatments

Choose lippings to suit your design. To minimize chipped edges, ease the arris of a veneer-lipped panel with sandpaper or a hand plane after adding surface veneers. Thicker lippings can be chamfered, radiused or molded with a shaper or a router.

Solid-wood lippings

Mitered

Butted

Radiused

Veneered edges

Single veneer

Multiple veneers

Glue leather to wood molding.

Leather edges

Attach thick molding with a spline.

Leather-wrapped miter

Glue leather-covered moldings to veneered substrates.

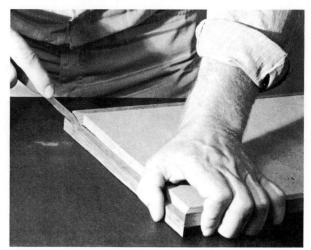

With the mitered lipping glued to the panel sides, use a marking knife to scribe the miters on the end lipping.

Fig. 2: Two ways to apply solid-wood lippings

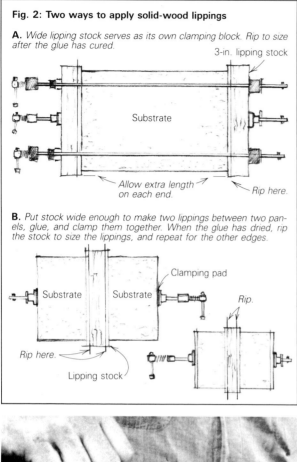

A. *Wide lipping stock serves as its own clamping block. Rip to size after the glue has cured.*

3-in. lipping stock

Substrate

Allow extra length on each end.

Rip here.

B. *Put stock wide enough to make two lippings between two panels, glue, and clamp them together. When the glue has dried, rip the stock to size the lippings, and repeat for the other edges.*

Clamping pad

Substrate   Substrate

Rip.

Rip here.

Lipping stock

Spread an even coat of white glue on the substrate edge with a small paint roller before applying the lipping.

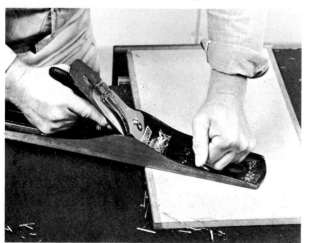

Rest the toe of the jointer plane firmly on the substrate to prevent tapering the lipping.

tried to glue on thin lipping (figure 2). After the lipping is glued onto the panel, you can quickly cut it to width. The lipping stock should be just slightly thicker than the substrate, at most $\frac{1}{16}$ in. more on each side. You could make it the same thickness as the panel if you could position it exactly when you glue it on, but this is difficult. Leave a small amount on each face and plane it flush after glue-up. The lipping need be only $\frac{1}{16}$ in. or so overlong at each end. Don't try to buy insurance by leaving excessive amounts of wood everywhere. It's tough to remove before you glue on the veneer.

The key to spreading a thin, even coat of glue on the substrate edges and the lipping is to use a narrow paint roller (the bubble pack it comes in makes a good reusable glue tray). You don't need any exotic joinery to secure the lipping: once the lipping is glued on, it's never going to come off in conventional use. In fact, I once put lipping on without glue—I just pinned it, leaving the pins proud so that I could remove them. I veneered the top and bottom, then took the pins out. Try as I might, I couldn't break the lipping off.

White PVA glue is fine for both veneer and lipping. Don't put excessive amounts of glue on either surface. Remember, you're going to have to deal with the accrued amount from both of them coming together. All you've got to do is wet the surface with glue. If the surface has dry patches, it won't adhere. If you put on too much glue, you'll get dribbles and they'll be a problem when you trim the lipping, whether with a router or a plane. All you want visible are little beads of glue. If you trim this lipping with a router trimming bit, the bit's pilot needs to travel on an absolutely clean surface, otherwise it will hit glue bumps and won't flush the lipping. If the pilot has a clear path, you can set the bit to no tolerance and clean the lipping perfectly.

The alternative is to plane off the excess lipping by hand, using a jointer plane. Clamp the panel to the bench. Put the toe of the plane on the surface and plane in a circular motion across the grain, with the substrate acting as a register for the toe. Careful, though—once the plane gets down to the substrate, stop. Don't remove lipping by planing straight along the grain. It's too easy to tip the plane and taper the lipping. Planing across, rather than with, the grain gives you a slightly less smooth surface, but that doesn't interfere with the gluing on of veneer. The thing you've got to guard against is lifting the plane's toe off the substrate, else you'll lose the absolutely flat surface. Keep a straightedge handy to check your work. Clearly, it's bad practice to glue on the lipping with $\frac{1}{4}$ in. of excess on each side, or to put it on high at one point and down at another. It's easy to get it on, but you pay the price when you have to remove the excess. Nothing other than care and accuracy will do. Cleaning up the lipping is not done rapidly. You can't do it accurately with a belt sander.

Once the lipping is absolutely level with the substrate, the panel is ready for veneering. If you're not going to veneer right away, cover the panel to keep off dust and contamination. Contrary to an old popular practice, there's no need to scuff the surface with a toothing plane; glue doesn't need a rough surface to work. The surface is now as flat as it's ever going to be—scuffing will only ruin it.   □

Ian J. Kirby is an educator, designer and cabinetmaker. He operates Kirby Studios in Cumming, Ga. Drawings by the author. For the remaining articles in this series, see pp. 14-18 and pp. 20-24.

Getting on the good side of veneer

Veneers come in three types: sawn, sliced and rotary-cut. Sawn veneer is the oldest form, and was very common in Europe in the 1700s. It's simply a piece of wood, any thickness up to ⅛ in., sawn from a log or a board and then planed. Sawn veneer hasn't been used much in recent years, though modern band resaws offer a good chance for its revival, especially since any wood can be sawn into veneer. Modern resaws saw wood thinly and accurately, and because they make a very fine kerf, thus minimizing waste, they're economical, too.

Rotary-cut veneer, which generally is confined to the manufacture of plywood, is made by mounting a whole log on a giant lathe and peeling off veneer as if it were wallpaper. It's rarely used as a surface, show-wood veneer in furniture, although it can look nice, as in some birch plywoods used for drawer bottoms and carcase backs. Rotary-cut veneer can be very thick (⅛ in.) or very thin. Only diffuse-porous woods that grow abundantly in plywood-manufacturing areas, such as lauan in Southeast Asia and birch in Europe, are rotary-cut.

Woodworkers are most concerned with sliced veneer. Any wood can be sliced: hard, soft, ring-porous, diffuse-porous, fast-grown, slow-grown— it doesn't matter. Essentially, a guillotine-type knife is brought down through a block of wood to slice off thin pieces, usually ½₂ in. to ½₈ in. thick. The veneer doesn't lose any measurable thickness during drying. Veneers can be sliced thinner, but I find that ¼₀ in. is about the thinnest that can be handled easily in a small shop.

Sliced veneers are most commonly available in 6-ft. to 8-ft. lengths, the size of most slicing machines, but lengths of up to 16 ft. can sometimes be found. Widths of up to 30 in. are possible, but getting a wide piece of veneer doesn't have the same attraction as getting a wide piece of wood does. It's easy to cut, match and join veneers together to create the widths and grain patterns needed for any job. Wide veneers frequently are rougher and coarser in the center than on the edge, so they can be difficult to smooth and finish.

Veneer-cutting technology is complicated, and the only thing that most woodworkers need to understand is that there is considerable cracking of wood tissue during the slicing process

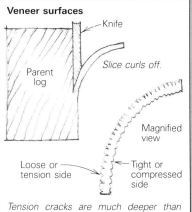

Veneer surfaces

Knife

Parent log

Slice curls off.

Magnified view

Loose or tension side

Tight or compressed side

Tension cracks are much deeper than compression cracks, since the tension side is stretched more as the slice curls.

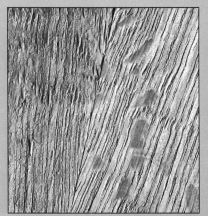

Bookmatching shows the difference between compression and tension surfaces. Compression side, right, has more sheen and is smoother than tension side.

Veneer bent along its grain with the tension side up will bend a great deal without audible cracking. With the compression side up, the radius of the curve will be greater and you'll hear cracking before the piece actually breaks.

and the two sides of each veneer piece will have very different characteristics. Two different surfaces are created as each new slice curls off the parent log, as shown in the drawing. (For more about knife checks, see the article on pp. 4-6.)

This difference is important when you're deciding which side to glue to the substrate. By putting the smoother compression side up (the tight side), you'll have the more cohesive side of the veneer on the outside, with the deeper cracks of the tension (loose) side against the substrate. Smooth-side-up is best for hand-woodworking, because when you clean and sand you will go through the small compression cracks and get to the solid part of the veneer much more easily.

These two surfaces also affect bookmatching. If you have a highly figured veneer 6 in. wide and you want a 12-in. panel, you might be tempted to open two consecutive pieces like a book and put them together so that the pattern matches down the center (you can do this since veneers are stored in bundles or swatches in the order in which they were sliced). This works in solid wood, but with veneer you expose one tight side and one loose side. The visual effect when finish is applied to bookmatched veneers can be quite poor. A surface that looks fine all through the process suddenly takes on a different feel, because the tight and loose sides will absorb the finish differently and that makes the surfaces reflect light differently.

There are several ways to tell which side is which. You can rub the surfaces with your hand—the loose or tension side will be rougher. Or you can look at the stuff, and generally the side that looks smoother is the tight or compression side, and it will have more sheen than the loose side. Neither of these methods is reliable, though. The best way to differentiate between the two sides is to bend the veneer and imitate what was happening to it when it came off the machine. With the tension side up, it will bend sharply without any audible or visible cracking. If you turn it over and do the same thing on the other side, you'll feel greater resistance and hear cracking. Thus the side that is less prone to bending is the compression side; the other is the tension side.   —I.J.K.

Laying Veneer
Meeting the small shop's pressing needs

by Ian J. Kirby

Furnituremaking with solid wood is like whittling: you chip away at the tree until you end up with the pieces you need. Working veneer is just the reverse: you stick the bits together to build up furniture elements of the exact size and shape you want. This means you have to think about the work in a different way—you have to plan ahead instead of making dimensional decisions as you go along.

This difference in thinking is in fact the most difficult aspect of veneering. The work itself, the techniques, is well within the skills, tools and budget of the small-shop woodworker. And, you'll find that veneering has three distinct advantages for furnituremaking: you can make panels of any size; you can use woods of rare beauty; and, a design bonus unique with veneered panels based on dimensionally stable substrates, you don't have to allow for moisture-related wood movement, as you would with solid wood.

Any veneered panel is assembled from three components: a substrate or base material, some lipping or edge treatment, and the veneers themselves. Preparing the substrate is the first step, but this is relatively easy with ordinary woodworking tools and dimensionally stable medium-density fiberboard (MDF) or furniture-grade particleboard. For the photos to illustrate this article, I used a piece of ⅝-in. MDF about the size of a cabinet door or small tabletop, and glued a mitered lipping of solid wood onto its edges. This way, the edges can be radiused or shaped in some way, and the finished piece will have the look and feel of solid wood. (For an article on preparing substrates and attaching lippings for veneering, see pp. 10-13.) Once you've glued on the lippings and planed them flush with the surfaces of the substrate, you're ready to apply the veneers.

Normally pieces of veneer are taped together to make sheets as wide as the panel. Veneers commonly are available in lengths up to 8 ft., so usually it's not difficult to find

A must-have for veneer work is a press to hold the veneers to the glued substrate while the glue cures. On Kirby's combination veneer press/woodworking bench, flat torsion boxes form the bed and top cauls; bar clamps and cambered battens apply the pressure.

pieces as long as your panel. For very long panels or for special effects, you can join several pieces to make strips as wide as the panel, then end-join the wide strips to make one long sheet. Veneers are easy to cut and join, so you have considerable design freedom here. Books on traditional veneering usually illustrate a variety of patterns, such as bookmatched mirror images or herringbone patterns, but these patterns are somewhat old hat and unnecessarily restrictive. You can match and join veneers in any way you like to create any type of pattern that appeals to you. The only rule for joining veneers is visual—what does it look like? Use your imagination. Experiment with combinations of grain directions and angles, with different species, and with bands, circles and other shaped inlays. Try aligning the grain or color of the veneer so that it accents the lines of the piece you're making.

No matter how much cutting and taping is done, the aim is to prepare a single veneer sheet that's no more than ½ in. larger all the way around than the panel to which it will be glued. A bigger overhang would just get in the way. Covering the entire panel at once enables you to make the veneer joints virtually invisible, without having to cope with glue squeeze-out between pieces, and to position the sheet accurately before placing the panel in the veneer press.

Both sides of the substrate must be veneered, usually at the same time; otherwise, the panel will be unbalanced and will invariably cup. The cupping results from a complex interaction of the glue, substrate and veneers, and from the shrinkage of

When crosscutting veneer, make two hard passes with a sharp knife, then press down on the straightedge while pulling the veneer up to break along the scoring (top photo). A veneer saw, guided against a board, is better for fragile veneers.

these components due to moisture changes. You should use a similar species and thickness of veneer on both sides of the panel to maintain a balance. Don't expect a thin, porous veneer to balance a thick, dense one.

For top-notch work, it's common to glue two layers of veneer on each side of the panel. The first veneer, the underlay, is usually an easily worked, mild species such as Honduras or African mahogany. This layer helps prevent the lippings from telegraphing through, and seems to give a richer, more solid feel to the work. Once the underlay has cured and been cleaned, it's covered with a show-wood veneer—anything from a burl or crotch to some exotic species such as ebony. Normally the top veneer is laid with its grain at right angles to that of the underlay veneer. If the top veneer and the underlay are different colors, lip the underlay with a 1-in. to 2-in. band of the top veneer, unless you want this color difference to highlight the edge.

With a fragile material such as burl or crotch veneer, it's common practice to reinforce the delicate material by gluing it onto a thick underlay veneer such as poplar. Those new to veneering should avoid very delicate materials, however, as well as old, cracked or washboard-like veneer, until they have mastered the techniques and gained more experience. There are ways to reconstitute badly buckled veneer, such as pressing it between damp layers of paper to flatten it, then slowly drying it to the proper moisture level, but these techniques can be troublesome and undependable. There are so many types of veneer readily available today, you can save yourself a lot of trouble by buying high-quality, flat veneer to begin with.

Other than conventional woodworking tools, all you'll need to begin veneering are a veneer press (see box, p. 18), a shooting board (as shown in drawing, p. 16), a glue roller and some veneer tape, which is available from most veneer suppliers. You could buy a veneer trimmer, which is a wooden knife-blade holder that looks like a handsaw handle, but a chisel and a knife work well to start with. A sharp knife (a Swiss Army knife is ideal) is good for cutting veneers, but for some hard and tough veneers, you might want a veneer saw, which has a barrel-shaped, serrated blade with no set. Oddly enough, this is also a handy tool for cutting very fragile veneer, such as burl.

Once you've assembled all your tools, you're ready to select, mark out and cut the veneers. To avoid damaging the workbench, cut on the wide surface of the shooting board. To crosscut veneer, hold the knife firmly against a metal straightedge (use the back for cutting to avoid damaging the accuracy of the chamfered edge), press hard as you cut, and chop down when you get to the second edge to prevent splintering. Make two hard passes, then break the scored veneer along the straightedge. The cut end will be slightly ragged, but that doesn't matter if it will be part of the waste overhang. If you want to join veneers end-to-end, however, knifing all the way through the veneer will produce a good joint line. It's rarely necessary to plane end grain.

When cutting along the grain, knife all the way through. Make light strokes, keeping the blade vertical and tight against the straightedge. These knifed edges are not good enough for a butt joint, so you'll have to true them with a jointer plane on the shooting board before you can tape them together.

If the veneer is mild and flat, you can plane up to a dozen

For butt joints, the sheets of veneer must be straight-edged. Hold the veneers in place on the shooting board while truing the edges with a jointer plane.

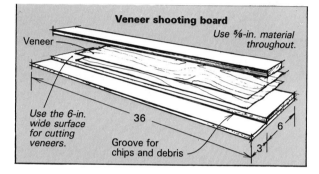

Veneer shooting board

Use 5/8-in. material throughout.

Veneer

Use the 6-in. wide surface for cutting veneers.

36

Groove for chips and debris

6

3

sheets at once; if it's anything but flat, two may be the limit. To use the shooting board, lay the plane on its side and position its sole 1/8 in. from the shoulder of the rabbet, then move the veneers to the sole. Line up a piece of wood with the rabbet shoulder and hold the veneers down by pressing hard on the top board. You'll be able to see only the top veneer, so you'll have to gauge from the shavings whether you're planing all the sheets. The amount of material removed is small, usually not enough to significantly affect bookmatching or any other pattern you're striving to achieve. When you think you've planed through all the chipouts and wavering edges, split the package apart and check the edges. If there isn't a good edge on each sheet, put the package back together and repeat the procedure.

If the edges look true, you can test the joint by putting two veneer edges together and using your fingers to press down the veneers as you check individual points along the joint. The points should come together perfectly, with no gaps. If the joint is tight at each checkpoint, it likely will be tight along its entire length. You may not be able to put the whole joint together at once, as you would with solid wood, because buckles in the veneer can distort the edges once the veneers are released from the shooting board. Pressing the edges flattens them out as they were on the shooting board.

If you're satisfied with the joint, you're ready to tape the veneers together. Veneer tape looks like brown packing tape, but it's much thinner and stronger. Don't use the thicker packing tape or masking tape, which can cause depressions in the veneer when it's pressed. Tape the top or face side only—

never put the tape between the veneer and the substrate, as the tape will show through and it may delaminate.

When taping, the joint is first pulled tight by strips of tape placed at right angles to the joint line. A single long strip placed over the joint helps hold the pieces together and prevents glue from oozing through during pressing. Tear the tape into 5-in. to 6-in. strips, which allows about 3 in. of tape on each side of the joint. Tear the tape—don't cut it—so that you have a feathered edge which is unlikely to mark the veneer. To join flat veneers, place the tape strips 9 in. apart; on buckled pieces, put them 2 in. to 3 in. apart, or as the material demands. First moisten the tape with a damp sponge—warm water on the sponge will make the glue grab a little better, which helps with oily woods such as teak. Attach one end of the tape to the first piece of veneer, pressing hard to make it stick. Then, holding the joint together with one hand, pull hard on the tape to stretch it slightly and attach it to the second veneer. After all the cross tapes are on, put a length of tape over the joint line, leaving the tape about 1/4 in. to 1/2 in. short at each end so that you can check if the joint is tight. At this stage you could run a wooden roller over the tape strips to make sure they're secure. I've never found a

To temporarily join veneers into sheets, stretch pieces of veneer tape across the seams on the face side. The tape keeps the veneers from moving around in the press.

Finish the edges of the veneered panel with a jointer plane, after first trimming with a veneer trimmer, router or knife.

roller to be a vitally important tool, but it's something you should try for yourself.

There are two methods of applying veneer to the substrate: hammer-veneering by hand, or by using a veneer press. Hammer-veneering isn't really done with a hammer but with a squeegee-like tool that presses down the veneer onto a substrate covered with hot hide glue. The glue holds when it coalesces, and the trick is to be pressing on the veneer when the glue grabs. This isn't a skill that can be acquired on the first try, or even the second. Dealing with more than a few square feet of veneer compounds the problem—I think you will find a veneer press to be a much more efficient alternative.

If you use some form of press, any of the modern cold-curing glues work well. White PVA glue is cheaper than yellow glue, and it doesn't set up as quickly, so there is more time to prepare the panels. It will cure in the press in three to four hours, depending on temperature. Urea-formaldehyde glue (such as Weldwood Plastic Resin) can be used, although it takes at least five to six hours to cure at 65°F. Don't use contact cement—it is absolutely out of the question. Contact cement remains elastic and doesn't harden the way woodworking glues do. It is also more prone to attack by the solvents in some finishes.

With a paint roller, apply a thin, even coat of glue to the substrate only. Don't put glue on the veneer, or it will curl and be difficult to control. On a properly glued panel, only little beads of glue will be squeezed out all around the edges. If you apply too much glue, it will be pressed through the veneer's pores and the surface will be glazed. If this happens, the panel isn't ruined—the glue can be cleaned off, so it won't affect the finish—but it will take a lot of work planing, scraping and sanding to remove the glazing. Gauging the amount of glue required is a matter of experience. You'll find that different substrates will soak up different quantities of glue.

Place one sheet of veneer taped-side-down on the bench, and after covering one side of the substrate with glue, position it on the veneer. Apply glue to the second side of the substrate and place the second piece of veneer on it, taped side up.

If the joint line has to be centered, pencil a centerline on the edge of the substrate before you begin, then align your mark with the joint line. If precise alignment isn't important, position the veneer by gauging the overhang with your fingertips.

The panel must be placed in the press so that pressure first hits along the panel's centerline and then spreads out to the edges. The spreading pressure prevents glue from being trapped in the center of the panel. If excessive amounts of glue remain trapped in the center, the veneer can ripple.

When the panel is taken out of the press, the first thing to do is determine if there are any unglued areas. To check for bubbles, which are usually caused by a lack of glue, tap the panel with your fingernail—there'll be a change in tone where the veneer has lifted. To reattach the veneer, slit into the area with a thin-blade knife, ease in glue with the blade or a syringe, and clamp the section down.

The next step is to remove most of the excess veneer from the panel edges with a veneer trimmer, a trimming bit in a router, or a knife. The greater the excess overhang, the more difficult this process becomes. In any case, what you're trying to do here is to get close; the final edge is achieved by planing. If the edge is to be radiused or shaped, do it now.

At this point, the veneer tape should be removed. One way to do this is to moisten it, give the water about two to three minutes to soften the glue, and pull off the tape. Running an ordinary household iron over the moistened tape also makes it easier to remove. Be careful with water; don't use too much, and try to keep it on the tape so that it doesn't spread onto the veneer. Don't wash off the residual glue left by the tape—blot up excess water with paper towels as soon as the tape is removed and let the area dry before proceeding.

The final cleanup is done by planing, sanding or scraping, or a combination of the three. Careful use of a sharp, finely set jointer plane produces the best surface. Not all veneers will plane, however, and you can't make sweeping generalizations about which species can be planed. You'll have to experiment with each batch of veneer you use. If you sand from start to finish, start with 180-grit, followed by 220-, then

Bench-pressing veneer

A veneer press must have an extremely flat bed and some system for selectively applying pressure to a panel. The press I've designed, and for which I have applied for a patent, uses three torsion boxes: one acts as the bed of the press and the other two are movable cauls that go over the veneer assembly before it's pressed. The torsion boxes are made by gluing fiberboard skins over core strips on 7½-in. centers; the voids between the strips are filled with resin-coated-paper honeycomb. A torsion box is very flat, stable and strong. Because of the way it's made, of course, it is also remarkably light.

Pressure is applied to the veneered panel with a series of clamps and cambered battens (detail A). The cambered side of each batten is oriented toward the panel. One batten is placed on top of the caul, another is placed under the bed, directly below the top batten, and the clamps on each end are tightened. Because the battens are cambered, they transfer the pressure from the center first to the outside edges as the clamps are tightened in unison.

Place the panels in the center of the press on a platen, a ⅛-in. thick fiberboard plate treated with wax so that residual glue can be removed. The veneer and substrate assembly must be in the middle of the platen and sandwiched between it and a second platen. Now add the top caul and battens. It's easy to assess how close to put the battens. As shown in detail B, clamping pressure is diffused in a fan of about 90° from the clamp head. Use enough clamps to ensure that the pressure fans overlap. If both top cauls are used with the bench shown here, ten battens are needed: five each on top and bottom (an equal number on top and bottom helps prevent bowing.)

Once the battens are in place, tighten the clamps enough to put a little pressure on the battens. By looking at the gaps between the battens and caul on each side of the centerline, you can make sure you're applying pressure equally. Continue to tighten the clamps on each side until you see the battens flatten out over the area being pressed. You can sense the same amount of pressure coming through the clamp bars.

Don't overtighten the clamps, especially if the panel you're veneering is narrow. If overtightened, the caul will bend around the edges of the panel and leave an area of low pressure or no pressure in the panel center. The glue will migrate to the low-pressure area and the veneer will ripple as it dries. To avoid this washboard center, use a straight-edge to check the top edge of the caul to make sure it doesn't become convex as you tighten the clamps. Also, when pressing narrow panels, place dry spacers the same thickness as the veneered panel on each side of the panel to help prevent the caul from bending. —I.J.K.

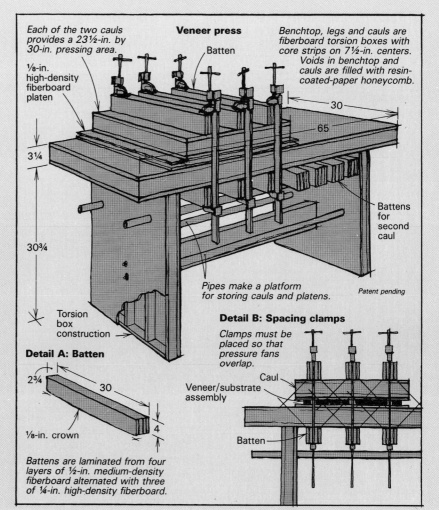

Each of the two cauls provides a 23½-in. by 30-in. pressing area.

Veneer press

⅛-in. high-density fiberboard platen

Benchtop, legs and cauls are fiberboard torsion boxes with core strips on 7½-in. centers. Voids in benchtop and cauls are filled with resin-coated-paper honeycomb.

Batten

3¼

30

65

30¾

Battens for second caul

Pipes make a platform for storing cauls and platens.

Patent pending

Torsion box construction

Detail A: Batten

2¾   30

⅛-in. crown   4

Battens are laminated from four layers of ½-in. medium-density fiberboard alternated with three of ¼-in. high-density fiberboard.

Detail B: Spacing clamps

Clamps must be placed so that pressure fans overlap.

Caul

Veneer/substrate assembly

Batten

300- or 400-grit. Avoid wet-or-dry paper—the dark abrasives can cause unsightly smudges on light woods. Be careful when sanding, especially near the edges. An awful lot of bad things happen when people let loose with a sanding block or a power sander. Check the edges frequently with a straightedge to make sure you aren't softening or rounding the area 1 in. to 2 in. from the edges. Rounding the edges with a sander is the hallmark of the careless. It shows dramatically once the work has been polished as a lack of crispness and cleanness. It's not easy to describe—it's just a sloppy look about the whole thing. The scraper, to me, is the crudest of cutters—it's difficult to scrape without marking the veneer wherever

the scraper is put down or taken off the panel.

Any finish can be used on veneered panels, but the solvents used in the finish may attack the glue. The first coat of finish should be applied sparingly, especially if you're using polyurethane or another material with a great deal of solvent. Applying one or two thin coats creates a barrier against solvents. After the thin coats, proceed as you would with solid wood. □

Ian J. Kirby, a designer, cabinetmaker and educator, operates Kirby Studios in Cumming, Ga. For more on hammer-veneering, see the article on pp. 25-27. For Kirby's article on preparing substrates, see pp. 14-18.

Drawings: Keith A. Bushee

Inventing Marquetry

I was an oil painter for seven years before I discovered marquetry. Between paintings I carved wood and worked with veneers. Around 1975 I hit on what I thought was an original idea: using the natural warmth and beauty of veneers to create pictures. I called them "wood pictures" because I'd never heard of marquetry. Then I saw in the Spring '76 issue of *Fine Woodworking* that I'd not invented the ancient art of marquetry (see pp. 60-65). A visit to the library enlightened me as to its history and methods. Like me, the author of the book I read had also first felt he had invented a new art form.

My tools consist of X-acto knives, rigid, single-edge razors and chisels. Most of my pictures I construct by applying one piece at a time to particleboard using a nonlatex contact cement. I start at one end of the picture and work across to the opposite end, making sure each piece blends with and complements the overall picture. Though the artist and paint-mixer still thrive within me, I do not paint or stain any part of my pictures. I do burn in fine lines and details.

I was born and raised on Chicago's South Side, and I'm most interested in both city and country scenes. My pictures come from sketches of images in my mind, though I will use the camera too. Marquetry is more difficult than painting, but I find that being limited to the natural hues and tones of wood is a challenge. —*Jim Davis, Hoffman Estates, Ill.*

Above, 'South Side' displays an avodire sky and a walnut burl Lake Michigan. The steel mills and factories are of rosewood, maple and sycamore. There are more than 300 veneer pieces in this picture, 18 in. by 24 in. In 'Golden-Gate Bridge,' top, 12 in. by 18 in., a vermilion tower looms behind hills of walnut burls, quarters and crotches. The road is rosewood and the cables are burned into the hills and sky. Left, 'Powerhouse,' 12 in. by 24 in., composed from a photo, is mainly sycamore (sky) and bubinga (foreground).

Designing With Veneers

Illusion can be as strong as structure

by Ian J. Kirby

There's more to veneering than technique; in fact, the essence of veneering is design and actually using the material to create real furniture and pleasing visual effects. The various buffet tables shown here are the result of class problems aimed at developing the design and craft skills of students at my school near Atlanta. A look at how these students handled the assignment shows you what is possible with veneers, and also gives you a glimpse at the whole process of designing.

The students already had learned to make torsion boxes and to handle basic veneering techniques, but some of them had never attempted a major piece of furniture. The buffet therefore seemed an ideal first project. It has a simple form and function—a food counter when a buffet meal is being served—but since it just stands idle in a room most of the time, it must also be an attractive piece of furniture. After discussing these requirements, I recommended that the students start with a basic table form and make it elegant by varying the proportions of the components. Then, if they could enhance their design with the visual

Five different veneers—padauk, ebony, African walnut, makore and pecan—used in proportion to their visual intensity create an eye-catching highlight on the top of de Alth's buffet.

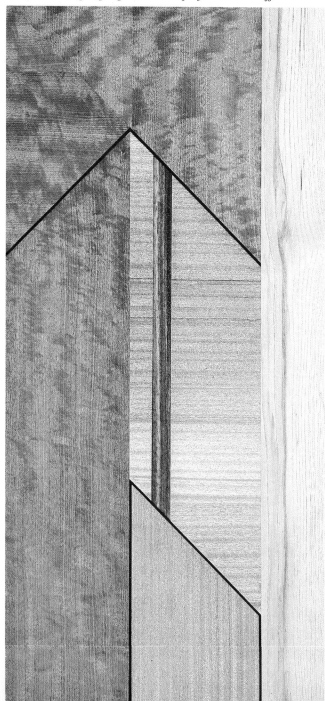

Carefully joined sections of veneer make George de Alth's buffet appear to be assembled from blocks of solid wood, rather than from sheets of medium-density fiberboard.

Photos: Gary Bogue

details that can be created with veneers, they would be well on the way to successful pieces of furniture. Torsion boxes (see the veneer press, p. 18) were included in the assignment because they capitalize on modern, dimensionally stable substrates to create strong structural elements with smooth surfaces perfect for showcasing the visual drama and movement of veneers.

Don't be put off by the apparent complexity of these designs. You don't have to be a trained designer to experiment with veneer arrangements and proportions. Everyone, whether he or she realizes it, has an eye for visual relationships. You can increase your awareness of these relationships by looking carefully and by thinking about what details make a piece of furniture work in terms of appearance or function. That's mainly what it takes—there's nothing magical about visual design.

One word of caution. Even though you may develop many good ideas for using veneers, don't immediately run off on some grandiose project. If you have never done any veneering, my advice is to make up two or three 9-in. by 12-in. practice panels, using mahogany or some other easy-to-work veneer; avoid anything that's badly buckled. Following the methods I've discussed in my previous articles (see pp. 10-13 and 14-18), prepare the substrate and apply the veneers. By the time you've finished the panels, you'll have learned enough to confidently use veneering technique on a real project.

As you study these pieces, you'll see two types of form: structural and visual. The torsion boxes establish the structural form of the buffets, and veneers create the illusion of form as they visually pull the components of the piece together. A good example of this type of visual unity is the buffet by George de Alth, shown on p. 20, in which he arranged the veneer grain patterns to flow from the top to the sides, linking the two surfaces into what appears to be one continuous, solid structure.

No amount of playing around with surface decoration or structural detail, however, will compensate for any miscalcula-tion in the basic proportions. Although proportion may be discussed as a mathematical concept, complete with formulas to guide you, it's mainly something you learn to sense and feel through practice and a great deal of drawing. There is no substitute for drawing—it's the most effective way to explore proportions and the interaction of line, pattern, color and other visual effects until you've created relationships that please you. The product of this work at the drawing board—a graphic design—is later translated into a three-dimensional structure, first a model, then a full-size piece. The model can be anything from a small-scale replica to a full-size mock-up, complete with colors or shapes pasted or taped on, but it should be as accurate as possible. Otherwise, you won't have any real feel for what the completed piece of furniture will be like.

The buffet by de Alth shows how a graphic design can be converted into veneers. By far the jazziest of all the pieces shown here, its visual power is concentrated within one area of the top. Five different veneers were used, each in proportion to its visual strength and color. For instance, the smallest area of veneer—5 sq. in. of ebony—acts as the highlight. It draws the eye right to it and has great impact.

In the teak and ebony buffet shown in the photo at right below, John Sherman developed a strong visual relationship between the top and the elliptical legs, which appear to be coming through the top. In reality, what shows is a piece of ebony veneer cut to the exact section of the leg. The illusion is compounded by ebony strips running across the edges of the top and down the legs, seemingly connecting the two pieces. The legs are oval torsion boxes. The ebony was veneered to a piece of bendable 3mm plywood, which was then glued onto the oval leg. Sherman's buffet also features inlay—a technique which is almost as old as veneering itself. In this case a teak and ebony laminate is inlaid around the edge of the top to highlight its shape. To accentuate this configuration even more, the ebony

A long strip of purpleheart ties the asymmetric form of Carter Sio's buffet table together visually (below left), while a veneer-deep illusion lets John Sherman's top grip his table's legs, which are oval torsion boxes.

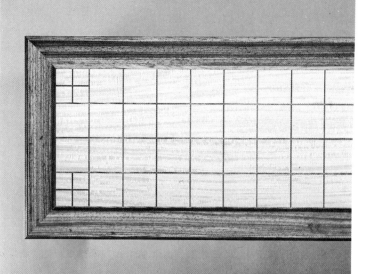

The mitered chamfer on Joe Wilson's padauk buffet is accentuated by satinwood inlay, which joins the chamfer, leg and top. Satinwood is also the primary wood in the raised window-like grid.

center panel mirrors the slightly bowed edges of the top.

Another example of how veneers can unify a piece is Carter Sio's buffet, shown in the left photo on p. 21. Although its form is asymmetric, the components are held together by a long band of purpleheart veneer.

Joe Wilson similarly united his padauk and satinwood buffet (photo, above) with a detail: a chamfer highlighted by a satinwood inlay. This makes clear the relationship between the parts—chamfer, leg and raised top—and gives the piece much of its power. The legs are joined to the top very simply with a ledger and pocket on the leg, as shown in the drawing at right.

The grid on the top of Wilson's table is formed by solid padauk strips inlaid into satinwood veneer, which is raised above the mitered padauk border. This might somewhat limit the use of the buffet, but Wilson decided that the visual effect gained was worth what might be lost in function. The pattern looks good and seems right because of its proportions. The side of the square equals the width of the border, the number of squares makes sense, and the small squares emphasize the corners. The success of this piece is the result of careful thought at the drawing board and many developmental drawings.

Scott Jenson's buffet (top photo, p. 23) is a good example of the selection and clever mixing of superb materials. The heavier pillar appears to be 5-in. rosewood cubes stacked one on top of the other. The effect is in fact created by applying the veneer so that every 5 in. the direction of the grain is turned 90°. This understated detail is discovered only when you get near the object, and then it comes as a surprise and a joy.

Jim Allen's buffet (bottom photo, p. 23) is a torsion-box structure built with medium-density fiberboard (MDF) skins over an MDF core. The principal veneer is fiddleback teak; the secondary veneer is rosewood. The legs are slightly thicker than

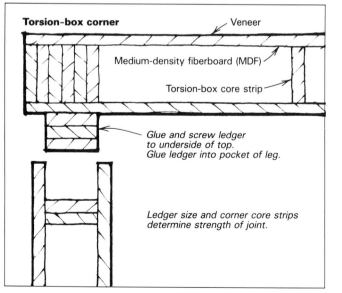

Torsion-box corner

Veneer

Medium-density fiberboard (MDF)

Torsion-box core strip

Glue and screw ledger to underside of top. Glue ledger into pocket of leg.

Ledger size and corner core strips determine strength of joint.

The larger pillar on Scott Jenson's glass-top table is veneered to look like a series of stacked 5-in. rosewood cubes.

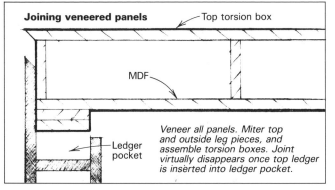

Joining veneered panels — Top torsion box

MDF

Ledger pocket

Veneer all panels. Miter top and outside leg pieces, and assemble torsion boxes. Joint virtually disappears once top ledger is inserted into ledger pocket.

the top, giving the piece a comfortable feel. (If the legs were the same thickness as the top, they would look spindly.) An interesting pattern is obtained by applying some of the fiddleback veneer at right angles to the grain direction of the main flow of veneer. On the top surface, the pattern is based on seven different-size rectangles, which create interest in the way that each juxtaposes to the next. The circle motif on the front edge is carried over the top, giving the illusion that the inlays are slices of a solid-wood cylinder. Circles also appear at the corners, where the rosewood veneer emphasizes the relationship of the legs to the top. There is a fairly important lesson to be learned here—the relationship of the parts, that is, the architecture of the piece, should be developed first. From these architectural lines come our first ideas about variations or decoration of the piece.

Allen worked within the architecture of the table to create illusions. How are the legs and top joined? Is the leg one piece, the top another piece, and the rosewood corner a third? What trickery holds the top to the leg, if the two pieces barely touch at the corners. Is there a tube of teak running through the center of the rosewood? To further suggest that the rosewood corner is a separate piece, Allen could have run a grooved line through the area where the rosewood contacts the teak. This would have created a shadow and a distinct gap on the surface.

Anybody can develop a sense of design. But keep in mind that complexity for complexity's sake is not good design. I find that new students tend to include their whole arsenal of techniques in each project, while more experienced workers generally refine a theme, then develop it fully. You should be aware of this difference as you start thinking about design. With attention to detail and practice, you can make your first major piece of veneered furniture something special. □

Ian J. Kirby is a designer, cabinetmaker and educator in Cumming, Ga., where he operates Kirby Studios. His first two articles in this series are on pp. 10-13 and 14-18. Drawings by the author.

Jim Allen's table, below, appears to be inlaid with slices of solid-wood cylinders.

Matchmaking

A good way to begin designing with veneers is to imagine that you are a graphic designer working with lines and color, pattern and rhythm, rather than a woodworker dealing with bits of wood. Veneer is so rich and varied that you can design in much the same way as an artist paints, with an entire palette of visual effects to accent, define or enrich a piece of furniture.

As you begin matching veneers, you'll find that the variations are almost endless—certainly there are more combinations than the conventional bookmatch, slipmatch and herringbone patterns you see diagramed in old veneering books. Such cataloging seems to indicate that there are rules or set patterns for veneering. Nothing could be further from the truth. When veneering, the only rules are visual, although you should realize that if you flip sheets of veneer you will have the tight side of one sheet next to the loose side of the next sheet (see explanation, p. 13). This will affect the looks of the panel when polished. There isn't a garish difference, but the two sheets will absorb finish differently and will reflect light differently. Other than that, don't be afraid to arrange veneer in any way you choose.

Figure 1 gives a glimpse of the kind of patterning that's possible. A single sheet of veneer is fairly uninspiring, unless it happens to be a particularly exotic species. Put it side by side with another sheet in a simple slipmatch (1A) and the effect is a little livelier. Arranging two consecutively cut veneer sheets to create a bookmatch (1B) is even more intriguing, but the four-sheet pattern in 1C just vibrates with life.

Finding good grain patterns for these more exotic matches takes a good eye and some careful searching. A simple but handy device is a homemade viewing window (figure 2A), which consists of stiff cardboard with a window cut to the shape and size of the sheet of veneer to be matched. It's quite extraordinary how grain and color come into focus when you isolate a section of a sheet through the window. Once you've found the section you like, you can find matching sections in the same position on successive sheets in the veneer stack and arrange them in a four-way match (2B).

To see what repeat-left, repeat-right or end-on-end matching will look like, hold a small mirror (an 8-in. by 5-in. mirror works well) at one end or edge of the window. If you want to see what a four-way match will look like, use two mirrors taped together to form a right angle (2C).

A pattern need not be complex to be

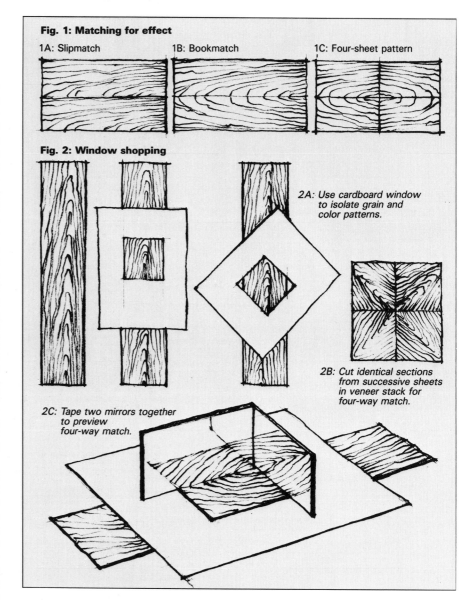

Fig. 1: Matching for effect

1A: Slipmatch

1B: Bookmatch

1C: Four-sheet pattern

Fig. 2: Window shopping

2A: Use cardboard window to isolate grain and color patterns.

2B: Cut identical sections from successive sheets in veneer stack for four-way match.

2C: Tape two mirrors together to preview four-way match.

eye-catching. A checkerboard, for instance, is a good example of the power of simplicity. The usual way to make a checkerboard is with alternating squares of light and dark veneers. An equally effective checkerboard can be made with only straight-grained ash squares assembled at right angles to each other. The result is dramatic, but somewhat more subtle than the usual black-and-white.

Another simple way to mix veneers is to use inlay and edgebanding. You'll find that a mix of approximately 90% major veneer with 10% inlay will generally create a pleasing effect. In these proportions, the alternate veneer acts as a highlight or color contrast to strengthen the shape or form of the object.

Veneer is available in a variety of thicknesses and species from local shops and mail-order houses. It's usually sold in bundles that have the sheets stored in the same order in which they were cut from the tree. Once you know the length and width of the veneer sheets you're buying, you can calculate the number of sheets required to give the pattern you want and the square footage you need. Since there are quite a number of variables here, including at least a 15% waste factor, it's usually impossible to get exactly the right amount, so it's best to buy extra. Otherwise, if you run out, you may be forced to use veneer from a different flitch, which could spoil the whole effect.

The best way to store veneer is to lay it on a larger board so there are no overhanging edges or ends that could get knocked and broken. Enclose the whole stack in an envelope of plastic sheeting to retain the moisture in the stack and to keep dirt out. Store the stack in a dark place—sunlight will rapidly fade veneer. Aging doesn't help veneer, but if the sheets are stored carefully, they can be saved for quite a few years.   —I.J.K.

Hammer Veneering
Veneer the whole world, without clamps

by Tage Frid

Hammer veneering is the old way of applying veneers to solid wood or to a plywood ground. The main tool is a veneer hammer, which is not used for hammering at all, but for applying pressure. The hammer has a very narrow face, so you can transmit the strength of your arms and the weight of your body to a tiny area of veneer. The veneer is held down by hot hide glue, which sticks as soon as it cools. You spread the hot glue on the ground surface and the veneer, then you use the hammer to squeeze it down tight before it cools. You can reheat the glue, and soften it, with an iron. Hammer veneering is usually the easiest way to fix old furniture with missing or broken veneers, or air bubbles under the veneers.

Hammer veneering is very fast to do, but the big advantage is that you don't need a veneer press or cauls or clamps. In regular methods of veneering, the size of the work is limited by the size of the veneer press or of the clamps. But with hammer veneering you could veneer the whole world if you wanted to. The same rules apply, however: When you veneer one side of a piece of wood, you have to veneer the other side too, or else the piece will be pulled concave toward the veneered side as the glue dries.

When veneering plywood, always cross the grain direction of the face veneer and of the ground layer. You can use some angle other than 90°, as long as the grain of the veneer and the grain of the top layer of plywood don't run parallel. If they are parallel, the veneer will crack later on. If your veneer

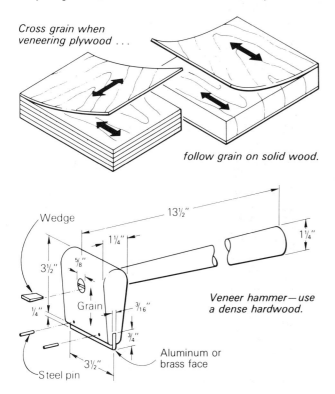

Cross grain when veneering plywood . . .

follow grain on solid wood.

Wedge — 13½" — 1¼"
1¼"
3½"
⅝"
¼"
Grain
3/16"
¾"
¼"
3½"
Steel pin
Aluminum or brass face

Veneer hammer—use a dense hardwood.

is applied to solid wood, be sure the grain does run parallel so the two layers of wood can move together.

Equipment

You will need a veneer hammer, a veneer saw, a hot glue pot (or double boiler), animal glue, a brush and an iron.

Veneer hammers vary in design, but usually have a long handle and a hardwood wedge for a head, with an inset aluminum or brass strip, which is the working face. The face must be straight and about 3½ in. wide, with a rounded profile to squeeze the veneer along a thin line. If you make your own hammer, follow the dimensions in the sketch and use a hard, heavy wood such as maple. Don't use steel or iron for the face, because it would react with the tannic acid present in most woods and cause a stain. Before using a new hammer, soak it in raw linseed oil so the glue won't stick to it.

A veneer saw or knife is used to cut the veneer to size. It is called both a saw and a knife because it is filed as a saw and

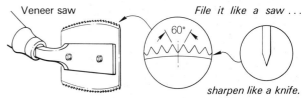

Veneer saw   *File it like a saw . . .*
60°
sharpen like a knife.

sharpened as a knife to make a smooth cut for edge-joining veneers. The curved blade of the saw is only about 3 in. long. Both sides of a veneer saw can be sharpened with a small triangular file. I file all the teeth at 90° to the surface of the blade, with no back or front, so that I can use the saw in either direction. This makes a slower but smoother cut.

After the teeth are filed sharp, the blade is sharpened so the cross section is like a knife, by rotating the saw along its curve against a stone. Hold the blade at a shallow angle, but be careful not to lose the points on the teeth.

A hot glue pot is a double boiler with a thermostat to prevent the glue from boiling. I don't use contact cement. I have seen too many failures, and it is just about impossible to repair. For large surfaces where veneers have to be edge-joined, contact cement could not be used. Contact cement has not been on the market very long, so nobody knows how long it will last. Hot glue is the oldest glue—it goes way back to the Egyptians. It is made from animal hides, bones and blood. It can be bought in dry sheets or as pearls. It must be soaked in water to soften it. Once it is soft, pour off any excess water. Then heat the glue in a glue pot or double boiler. Never put the pot directly on the heat source. It must always be over a pot of water. If hot glue boils it loses its strength, plus when it boils it doesn't smell like roses. When starting a new batch,

Tage Frid (silent g; rhymes with hey, kid) is retired professor emeritus of furniture design, R.I. School of Design.

melt the glue, let it cool and reheat it again and it will be ready to use. If the batch is already made up just heat it up and add water if it is too thick or let it heat for a while if it is too thin. Getting the right consistency is something you have to learn through experimenting. If the glue is hot all day its consistency changes constantly. If the consistency is right, the glue should drop from the brush like honey. You will know the glue is spoiled if it stays liquid after it cools.

To check that the glue is made correctly and is ready to use, put a drop between your fingers. Rub your fingers together, applying pressure. You should be able to squeeze out all the excess easily after about one minute if the room is around average temperature, 60° to 70° F. Your fingers should then start sticking together, because when hot glue gets cold it starts binding. The glue won't reach full strength until it dries completely, which takes about 24 hours.

Edge veneering

It is clumsy and time-consuming to veneer edges using clamps, but it is fast and easy to do it with the veneer hammer. It doesn't matter whether the edge is straight or curved. When you cut veneer, always have a flat piece of scrap wood underneath it to prevent cutting into the workbench, and use a straightedge to guide the saw. Cut strips of veneer only about ⅛ in. wider than the thickness of the work. If you cut them too wide, the excess sticking into the air will dry before the glue has cured and it will curl away from the wood.

When the veneer is cut, wet it on both sides to make it more flexible and also to see which way it naturally wants to arch. Glue it with the concave side toward the work, so the arch will keep it in place. If you do it the other way, it will be hard to keep the edges stuck down while the glue cures.

Begin by brushing glue onto the edge to be veneered, then turn the veneer over and lay what will be the outside surface right in the glue on the wood. Then brush glue onto the veneer. The glue that smears on the outside will help the hammer slide more easily. Later on you can scrape the veneer clean. Now flip the veneer over and hold it in place with one hand. Hot glue is very slippery. Hold the hammer in your other hand and press down hard to squeeze out the excess glue at one end. This will secure the veneer, and now you can put both hands on the hammer to squeeze out the excess glue all along the edge. You have to work fast to get all the veneer down while the glue is still hot. The minute the glue gets cold, the veneer will stick. Keep an old iron warmed up and handy. Then when you aren't fast enough, you can reheat the glue before going back with the hammer. Don't have the iron so hot that the glue burns, or you'll regret it. Burned glue makes an unpleasant stink that hangs around for a long time.

Use the veneer saw to clean off the extra glue and trim the veneer, while the glue is still soft. First dip the saw blade in hot water so it will be wet and warm and the glue won't stick to it. Then cut off the excess at both ends, holding the work up on an angle. After that, stand the work on edge and tilt it a little to apply pressure right at the corner, and saw off the excess veneer. Dip the blade in hot water after each cutting. Now put the piece aside to dry for about 24 hours.

It doesn't make any difference if the edge is curved or some other shape. Veneer it exactly as if it were straight. But when the work isn't straight, you must wait until the glue is hard and dry to remove the excess veneer and squeezed-out glue. Then use a block plane or a smooth plane to clean it off.

Wet the veneer to see which way it curls, then glue the concave side down, right, so the arch will help hold it in place.

Use the veneer hammer to squeeze out the glue all along the edge.

When trimming veneer, keep the saw warm and wet by dipping it in the glue-pot water. Stand the work on edge and tilt it a little to apply pressure, then draw the saw along the face of the board.

To trim a curved edge, let the glue dry hard, and plane.

Veneering large surfaces

To veneer a large surface, you will have to edge-join pieces of veneer either lengthwise or crosswise, or both. The edge joint must be very accurate. I ensure accuracy by overlapping the two pieces of veneer by about a half-inch at the joint, and after they are stuck down I cut through both pieces at the same time.

Begin by figuring out how you want the veneers to match and mark the location of each piece on the work. Then work on one section at a time. Wet the veneer and brush the hot glue onto the work. Place the moistened veneer upside down in the glue, exactly as when edge-veneering. Apply glue to the veneer itself, flip it over and put it in position, and use the hammer to secure it somewhere in the center.

Now use the warm iron to remelt the glue under a small section of the veneer. Push down with the veneer hammer as hard as you can, using the weight of your body, to squeeze out the excess glue. When that part is glued down, move to

Saw veneers to length with straightedge, backup board.

Lay veneer face down in glue. The glue that smears on it will help hammer slide easily.

With both sheets stuck and the seam trimmed, reheat with the iron and push hard with the hammer to squeeze the excess glue out through the line of the joint.

Lean your whole weight on the hammer, squeezing the glue toward the edges.

Saw through both veneers at once, carefully lift top sheet and peel away scrap beneath.

A hot iron remelts the glue in a troublesome spot. Then go over it with the hammer.

the next area. Heat the glue, press the veneer down, and proceed until the whole sheet is stuck tight. Work the hammer back and forth with the direction of the grain of the veneer, starting in the center of the width. But turn the face of the hammer at an angle so it will squeeze the excess glue toward the edges. Never work across the grain, as that would push the fibers apart and cause the veneer to crack when it dries.

Now apply glue to the next sheet of veneer and proceed in exactly the same way, making sure the edges to be joined overlap by about a half-inch. When they are both stuck, use a straightedge and a sharp, warm, wet veneer saw to cut through both sheets at once. Remove the scrap veneer from the top, then carefully lift up the top sheet and pull out the scrap from underneath. Then butt the edges together, heat with the iron, and push hard with the hammer to squeeze all the excess glue out through the line of the joint. When the joint is down tight, press a strip of heavy brown paper over the joint to prevent it from opening during drying. After the glue has dried, use a sharp scraper blade or a cabinet scraper to remove the paper and excess glue. (Turn the scraper's burr—the small hook running the length of the blade—heavier than normal.) A good seam should be invisible.

You must be sure there are no air bubbles under the veneer. If you can't find the bubbles when you push with the ham-

mer, tap the surface lightly with your fingernail and listen for hollow spots. If you don't get these hollow spots glued down, they will eventually crack. The veneer I used for these photographs was very curly in one spot in the center, and it would not stay down. So I heated the area to melt the glue, covered it with brown paper, and clamped a block of wood over the curly place to hold it down tight while the glue cooled and dried. If you don't notice the air bubbles until several days or months later, just apply water, heat and pressure to work the piece down. The glue will still hold. □

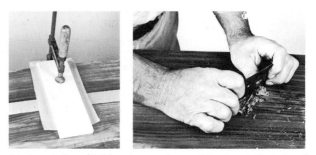

Block and clamp hold curly spot down while glue cools; strip of heavy paper along seam keeps it closed until glue dries. Then a sharp scraper cleans off paper and glue.

Tips on Veneering
How to avoid coming unstuck

by Tage Frid

Even the best veneering job can develop air bubbles, from uneven adhesion. Simply slice the bubble, inject glue and reclamp.

A poor veneer job will show up any mistakes in the most unforgiving way. Veneer can crack, bubble, curl up, or fall right off. This usually happens after the work has been delivered, which doesn't do your reputation any good. And repairing things often means refinishing the piece, a costly task. Everybody makes a mistake once in a while, but if you live long enough, like me, your mistakes can teach you how to correct some blunders before they happen.

In the first place, when you veneer over solid wood, make sure the grain in the veneer follows the grain of the board. Otherwise, as the board shrinks and expands, the veneer will loosen. When veneering plywood, run the grain of the veneer at right angles to the face grain. Don't try to veneer the end of any board thicker than ¾ in.—the veneer will eventually come loose. When veneering plywood edges, special care is needed. On veneer-core plywood, the core may telegraph through the edges as the wood moves. I double-layer edges where this will be noticeable, with the grain of the under layer of veneer running at 90° to the top layer.

In all cases, you must veneer both sides of a board, whether it's solid wood or plywood. Granted, some veneer is rare and expensive, and it seems a shame to veneer the back side when you know that it will never be seen. Yet if you don't, the piece will warp. You can use a cheaper veneer on the back than on the front, but only if both veneers are of similar density and will expand and contract at the same rate. I would never put maple on one side and poplar on the other, for instance, but I often use ordinary mahogany opposite expensive walnut. If in doubt, consult a table of expansion rates, such as that found in R. Bruce Hoadley's *Understanding Wood* (available from The Taunton Press), or the USDA's *Wood Handbook.*

The type of veneer should not make any difference in the procedure, except that both burl veneer and crotch veneer have to be flattened first to remove the bumps. I used to soak the veneer in a mixture of 2 parts Cascamite powder, 1 part flour, 3 parts water, 1½ parts glycerine and 1 part isopropyl alcohol. I can't get Cascamite anymore, so now I substitute Weldwood plastic resin. After soaking the veneer, I let it stand on end until it's dry to the touch, put layers of newsprint on both sides, and press out the bumps between two boards with a heavy weight on top. I change the paper after two hours and again after four hours, and then I allow the veneer to dry under a lighter weight for a day. It will be flat and ready to use when it comes out from between the boards. Leave it pressed flat until you need it. If it has dried out too much and become bumpy again, just moisten it with water and reflatten it.

Despite the flattening, burl and crotch veneer will eventually crack because the grain is going in all directions. This might take as long as 25 or 30 years, and as far as I know there is no way to prevent it from happening, but one trick to prolong the life of the job is to glue-size the veneer.

Sizing tricks—Glue sizing is a very thin, hot, animal glue applied to the wood in order to seal and stabilize it. The glue should always be heated in a double boiler, because if it boils it will lose its strength. It's impossible to give exact measurements for the amount of dry glue to mix in the water, as hot glue constantly changes as the water evaporates. But here is a way to tell if it's right: The glue should drop from the brush like heavy maple syrup, and by putting a drop between your fingers and rubbing them together with some pressure, you should be able to squeeze out all the excess glue easily. After about a minute, if the room is at 60°F, your fingers should start sticking together. With the glue in that condition, mix about 1 part hot glue to 2 parts hot water to make the glue size. Glue sometimes dries out. With luck, all you need to do is add water and reheat. But glue can go bad if it's too old. If it smells bad or turns liquid when it is cold, make a new batch.

Scrape the veneer and sand it with 80-grit sandpaper. Then apply the hot glue size to the surface and rub it in with the palm of your hand, wiping off any excess. When the glue is completely dry, usually after about 24 hours, scrape the veneer again lightly if necessary, then sand it. The glue sizing will not discolor the veneer or interfere with the finish. The process is worth the effort on all doubtful veneers, but glue sizing doesn't always work—rosewood will eventually crack whatever you do to it.

When veneering over end grain, apply one coat of glue size to seal the pores. Let it dry completely and then apply the veneer using hot glue, either hammer-veneering (see pp. 25-27) or clamping it. If the wood is soft, such as poplar or basswood, it's a good idea to size the ends twice.

Glue sizing is also a good way to repair cracked veneer when you're doing refinishing. Here the glue size should be thicker, about 1 part glue to 1 part hot water. Before you remove the old finish, force the glue size into the cracks with your fingers and the palm of your hand, rubbing hard. As the glue dries, it will pull down and reglue the veneer. When the glue is completely dry, remove the old finish with a cabinet scraper. Don't use any finish remover—it might dissolve the glue.

Gluing the veneer—There are many different glues on the market, all claiming they can glue everything except broken hearts. Some of them might work fine for veneering, if anybody wants to experiment. As for me, I wouldn't try a new glue on a real job without testing it first for a couple of years. I was put to the test recently when Cascamite, one of my favorite glues, disappeared from the market. In its place I

From *Fine Woodworking* magazine (September 1983) 42:74-75

now use Weldwood plastic resin, which had given me some trouble when I first tried it years ago. Now it seems fine. I never use contact cement on wood veneer. It doesn't really dry hard, so the veneer is liable to move and crack at any time. And the solvents in some finishes, such as lacquer or Watco, may cause the glue to loosen. Also, on large surfaces you will get air bubbles, and with contact cement, they are just about impossible to repair. I hope I've made all my gluing mistakes already, and learned something from them. My three standbys, depending on the type of job, are hot glue, Titebond and Weldwood.

I use hot glue for hammer-veneering. In this operation, pressure is applied by stroking the surface with a hammer shaped like a small squeegee. As the glue is squeezed out and cools, the veneer sticks flat. Then it can dry without clamping. This is a good technique for veneering the edges of panels, and will work even if you have used a different glue on the panel itself.

Even a dedicated clamper will find that hot glue has one feature that makes it ideal for certain jobs—it can be reactivated by heating. If you apply the veneer over glue that has cooled and then heat the job while it is in the press, the veneer won't absorb much moisture until the glue is reactivated. Thus it will not try to expand until after it has been firmly clamped down. This makes for a stabler job, because veneer that has been allowed to expand too much before clamping will always be under stress after it has dried, and will be more prone to cracking. Of course, you must have a way to heat the job in the press. Bags of sand can be heated and clamped with the work, a good trick for veneering curved panels, as the sandbag will conform to the curve and even out the pressure. For flat-press veneering, I heat ¼-in. plywood sheets and put them top and bottom—and between separate panels if I am doing a stack all at once. I also use ⅛-in. aluminum sheets for this; they hold the heat very well. To heat the sheets, I used to put them on the school radiators, which were always very hot. You could put them near a woodstove just as well.

Another advantage with hot glue is that the piece can be taken out of the press as soon as it has cooled enough, perhaps after a couple of hours. It won't have full strength for 24 hours, but it will be all right until then. Hot glue has one drawback, however. Because it reactivates, it is not good for humid and hot climates.

I use Titebond only when the work can be clamped up before the glue starts setting. The advantages of Titebond are that it is always ready, you don't have to mix it, it has a long shelf life, the brushes and rollers are easy to clean, and it is resistant to water and heat.

Weldwood plastic resin is my choice if there are a lot of pieces to be veneered or if the piece is big; its set-up time is longer, so I have more time to get the clamps on. It resists water and heat, but it has to be mixed, and then is usable for only a few hours. So don't mix a lot more than you need. When buying powdered glue, don't buy too large a can, because every time you open it moisture from the air gets in, and after a while the glue goes bad.

No matter which glue you're using, be sure that you put enough on and that it is evenly spread. But don't put so much on that it runs all over the work, the bench, you and the floor. You need just enough to allow a little to squeeze out along the edges. A good tool for spreading glue is a paint roller. Always leave a little extra glue along the edges, to be sure that they will stick down. Spread glue only on the surface of the piece to be veneered, never, never on the veneer. If glue is put on the veneer, the veneer will expand too much, and might crack later. Also, the wet side will expand more than the dry, causing the veneer to roll up like a scroll before you can press it.

Pressing—Before the job goes into the press, tack down the veneer so that it won't slide around under the pressure. Secure it in the center of each short-grain end. This will hold the sheet in place while still allowing it to expand. Tacked at the corners, the sheet would be trapped and it would wrinkle. After the first side is tacked down, cover the veneer with paper, so that if the glue comes through, the veneer won't stick to the press. Then glue and tack the other side.

If more than one piece of the same size is going to be veneered at the same time, put larger pieces of plywood between them. Never put the pieces to be veneered directly on top of each other. The surface would come out of the press very uneven, and if the pieces were not stacked exactly on top of each other, the edges would not be glued down.

When clamping, either with clamps or a veneer press, always tighten the center clamp first, then the others in the row that lines up with the grain of the veneer. Up to this point, from the time you started to apply glue, you should have been working as fast as possible. Now slow down. Give the glue a couple of minutes to squeeze out from the center toward the edges. Keep tightening the center row of clamps a little at a time until they are tight. Don't overdo it. Slowly follow up with the outer clamps, still starting from the center, then tighten everything down evenly. If you tighten the outside clamps too soon, the glue will be trapped and the veneer will buckle, and be likely to crack later.

As soon as the pieces come out of the press, clean their edges with a chisel while the glue is still flexible. When cleaning the end grain, use the back of a chisel to break the veneer over the edge, so it won't tear, then clean it.

After the edges are clean, stand the pieces on edge so that air can circulate all around them. If the pieces are left flat on the top of the bench, the sides exposed to the air will dry first, and the pieces will warp.

Testing for air bubbles—When the veneer is completely dry, tap the surface lightly with your finger and listen for hollow spots. It is very important to locate them and get them glued down, or else they will show up when the finish is put on and eventually they will crack. If you can't find the air bubbles by tapping with your finger, a sure test is to scrape and sand the surface, then dampen it with hot water, keeping it moist for a while. The veneer will absorb the moisture and expand, showing a bump wherever there is an air bubble. Mark the spot and let the veneer dry.

When the panel is thoroughly dry, slice open the air bubble with a sharp knife, cutting in line with the grain. I use a hypodermic needle to squeeze in some glue. Then I put paper and a block on, and clamp the repair. With hot glue, of course, you don't have to go through all this. To reactivate the glue, it's usually enough just to dampen the surface and iron down the bubble. □

Tage Frid is retired professor emeritus of furniture design, Rhode Island School of Design.

Oyster-Shell Veneering
Experimenting with sliced branches

by Girvan P. Milligan

When a branch from a tree is cut trans-
versely into thin slices and then applied to the surface of a box or piece of furniture, the grain and shape of the slices resemble
oyster shell. Hence the name of this traditional
decoration technique: oyster-shell veneering. Ernest
Joyce, in his fine book, *The Encyclopedia of Furniture
Making*, mentions the method, and that, along with the picture of a beautifully veneered cigarette box, led me to try my
luck oyster-shelling a small plywood box. An unproductive
plum tree provided wood with close grain, deep reddish
heartwood and creamy sapwood—most attractive for the purpose. A locust branch, ochre in the center, helped me discover more tricks of the trade.

Cutting round sections on the band saw is easier and safer
if you put a clamp on the branch or trunk to prevent rolling.
You can cut smaller branches on the table saw or radial arm
saw. Cutting diagonally rather than straight across yields oval
shapes, which look more like oyster shell. Also, angling the
cut varies the grain pattern though it also creates a problem in
grain direction, which must be taken into account in the final
scraping of the surface. I cut my slices freehand about ⅛ in.
thick and stack them with narrow spacers between. Joyce suggests weighting down the stack, and that works fairly well until you accidentally knock one over. Binding the stack with
strips of inner tube keeps the slices flat and permits easily
moving the stacks from one place to another.

Being thin, the slices dry quickly. I experimented with
burying the slices in dry sand, putting several thicknesses of
newspaper between them in the stacks, and clamping them
with cauls and no spacers or paper. The sand was the least effective because it provided no pressure and allowed the pieces
to cup and check badly. Short lengths of branch, however,
can be buried in sand with better results. Coating the ends of
the branches with glue also helps to reduce checking. I put
one of the stacks on top of the oil burner to hasten the drying
time—a lesson in patience. The stickered stacks that dried
more slowly in my cool shop produced more check-free slices,
though even the ones that did check with the other methods
gave much usable material.

When the "oysters" are dry you can cut them into squares,
rectangles, polygons or fit one to another in the more natural
curves of the round sections. In any case, the joints should be
hairline. Obviously, straight edges are easier to fit and keep
square; I use a shooting board and a block plane. Check the
fit of the joint by holding the pieces up to a bright light.
High spots can be cut down and checked again. In working
with curved joints you can sometimes chase high spots from
one end of the curve to the other since removing wood from
one spot changes the relationship of other segments of the
curve. Whatever the shape of the pieces, keep in mind the
size and shape of the surface to be covered so the finished

product will have a balanced pattern. You can bookmatch adjacent slices from the branch to start a pattern in the middle
and balance it with other matching pieces toward the edges.

When you've achieved a satisfactory fit, glue the pieces together one, or perhaps two, at a time. If the pieces are square
you can glue a whole row at once. One could lay out a whole
panel in jigsaw-puzzle fashion and glue it all at once, but
probably the joints will be tighter and assembly less nerve-
wracking doing it more gradually. Trials with adhesives including white glue, Weldwood, yellow glue and epoxy came
out in favor of "five-minute" epoxy. You can mix it in quantities small enough for each joint and its strength and speed
of setting enable the work to move along quickly. A board
covered with a piece of polyethylene and held in the vise is a
good assembly surface. Polyethylene releases any glue and ob-
viates the necessity of scraping off paper. Small clamps hold
the pieces in place while the glue sets and thus prevent warping. Clamp down all the edges and not just the joint: The
oysters tend to curl if not held flat. When you've assembled
an area large enough to cover the surface to be veneered, trim
the assembly a bit oversize and clamp or weight it between
cauls until you apply it to the surface. Some pieces of the
semifinished panels will be thicker than others. The radial
arm saw can cut down high spots and eliminate a lot of
laborious scraping. Just raise the sawblade up off the table a
distance equal to the thickness of the thinnest piece and pull
the saw over the piece repeatedly, shifting the panel between
pulls, until the panel is level.

Now construct a box to receive the assembled oyster-shell
veneers. Plywood offers a more stable base than solid wood,
multi-ply birch being the easiest to work. A box of ⅜-in. ply,
with the panels adding another 3/32 in. or a little less, does not
look clumsy and has adequate area for fastening hinges. My
joinery is simple. I rabbet the front and back of the box and
dado the sides, all of which I glue and nail together. The top
and bottom I butt-join, glue and nail. Because the veneer will
cover the entire outside, the joinery is concealed—any strong,
simple joint will do. The box has no opening yet; cutting off
the top is a later step.

Before gluing, coat the back of the panels with a thin layer
of glue and let it dry to increase the strength of the end-grain
glue bond. Trim each panel flush with the edges of the box.
When all the panels are glued and clamped in place and the
glue has set, scrape the surface level, taking care to scrape toward the center to avoid chipping the edges. When two

From *Fine Woodworking* magazine (November 1979) 19:66-67

obliquely cut pieces have been bookmatched, you can best handle the abrupt change of grain at mid-panel by scraping across both. A heavy power-hacksaw blade with the teeth ground off and all edges ground square makes an excellent scraper. It is 12 in. long, flexible and made of superior steel. Square grinding on a fine wheel gives an edge that holds, and its length provides the equivalent of half-a-dozen ordinary scrapers. When the section being used becomes dull, it is only a matter of moving down the blade a few inches to have a brand-new edge. And there are four edges. The edge that had the teeth remains a little wavy after they have been ground off, and this edge gives a rougher but faster cut. An old Victrola spring has also given me yards of excellent scrapers. A belt sander with an 80-grit belt will cut down the excess quickly, but take care to avoid burning the wood. In one trial with yellow glue, the heat of the sander softened the glue. Excessive heat can also cause checking and warping.

When you've completed scraping, cut a rabbet all around the top and on all four corners to accommodate a strip of edging the thickness of the panel. Cut the edging oversize, and scrape it down level with the surface. A contrasting color, either lighter or darker than the ground color, looks attractive. Narrow strips of inner tube wrapped about the box make satisfactory clamps for gluing the edging in place.

Now the whole box can be sanded to almost its finished state. There is more handling involved before completion, which may well result in scratches, so it is best to leave the final sanding till last. Cut the box open on the radial arm saw in its horizontal position, using a fine-tooth blade, or on the table saw. Take care to back up the corners with a piece of scrap to reduce the chance of splintering the edging. If you've used plywood for the box, line the box with either veneer or Formica. White matte Formica gives a nice light interior and can easily be kept clean. Veneer the exposed edges of the plywood along with the bottom of the box. I usually set four plugs made with a plug cutter into the bottom for short feet, which keep the bottom from becoming scratched.

Finish the sanding in good light, checking for the scratches you don't believe are there. They probably are. The final finish is to a large extent a matter of preference, but it's important that the surface be thoroughly sealed. Polyurethane is durable and with a number of coats and careful rubbing gives a beautiful result. Watco oil gives a nice finish, too, and allows for touching up mars more readily than polyurethane. Watco is not moisture-proof, however, and in one box finished with it there seems to be more expansion and contraction of the individual pieces.

Be prepared for wood movement. Cross-sectional pieces are highly sensitive to changes in moisture. Keep your finished boxes away from direct sunlight and radiators. To keep peeling and cracking to a minimum, cut the sections as thin as possible, size them before applying, and use a moisture-proof finish. You may still have to accept small cracks and gluelines that vary in size. I haven't tried the chemical wood stabilizer PEG (polyethylene glycol-1000); it might help.

A variation that is not truly oyster work (since the wood does not contain the heart) can be made from all those small scraps you have hesitated to throw away. Many woods have beautiful and interesting end grain, and careful matching and mixing can result in a handsome piece of work. □

Girvan Milligan, a retired teacher, lives in Carmel, N.Y.

Photos: Girvan Milligan

Branches sliced and stacked for drying. Weight, right, and strips of inner tube, left, keep oysters from warping.

Assemble oysters on a polyethylene-covered board, held in a vise.

Rabbet cut around top of box and corners receives edging. This box, veneered with assemblages of end-grain stock, is a variation on the oyster-shell technique.

Radial arm saw with fine-tooth blade cuts lid off box. Back-up board keeps veneer from splintering.

Marquetry and Veneer **31**

Patch-Pad Cutting

A basic method for cutting marquetry

by John N. Beck

The patch-pad method is one of several ways to cut and assemble wood veneers to form geometrical, floral or pictorial designs. The veneers are stacked between cardboard or plywood, and taped or tacked closed to form a "pad," which is then cut up with a jigsaw. This method has certain advantages. All the pieces are cut at once, and a single sawcut cuts the line between two adjacent pieces. (In some other methods each line is sawed twice.) Also, by using the cut pieces in different combinations, several pictures can be assembled from the same pad. In addition, by stacking sets of veneers, one can cut several identical pictures simultaneously. For the craftsman interested in selling his products, the time saved by this method is considerable. For the occasional marquetarian, there is no other method by which multiple cutting can be done.

The main problem of making wood inlay pictures is fitting the pieces. The patch-pad method accomplishes this to within the thickness of the saw blade used. No trimming of oversize pieces is necessary. Layers in the pad are made by taping choice veneers selected for specific picture pieces into cheaper veneer seconds called "wasters," to keep the layers even in thickness. The pad is sawed in a horizontal position with a vertical blade. Consequently, all edges are square and join precisely when butted together.

Cutting is the same with a hand or power jigsaw. I use a Rockwell Delta 24-in. throat, 1/3-horsepower jigsaw. If the picture is larger than the depth of the throat, the pad can be sawed into several smaller pads. An electric foot switch which

John N. Beck started marquetry shortly after coming to this country from Austria nearly fifty years ago, selling many pieces which he displayed in his Littleton, N.H., bakery.

turns the machine on and off leaves my hands free. Blade size is not determined by pad thickness, but by the size of the pieces to be cut. I usually choose a 4-0 jewelers' saw blade because the pieces in my pictures are generally small; for larger pieces a 2-0 is sufficient. I buy my blades from H. L. Wild, 510 E. 11th St., New York, N.Y. 10009. The blades are of high quality and break less than others.

The first requirement is a paper tracing of the desired picture. Two copies are needed: one is used as a master tracing upon which the names of the desired woods are indicated; the other is used for the assembly of the cutout pieces. A piece of acetate is cut to the exact size of the paper tracing, laid over the tracing, and the lines copied exactly with India ink to form a third picture template. This is called a "finder," helpful in choosing and orienting the grain patterns. All tracings should have 1/2-inch margins.

Two pieces of corrugated cardboard are cut to the exact size of the tracing. These form the top and bottom of the pad. On one cardboard the design is duplicated by tracing it over carbon or graphite paper with a ballpoint pen. This serves as the top of the pad.

In the picture shown here, I used a poor grade of maple for wasters. Any waste veneer will do providing it is the same thickness. The first piece in the pad is a poplar veneer chosen for its grain design which makes a perfect sky. I laid the finder (with the design tracing on it) over the poplar to select the most fitting grain pattern, and marked the finder edges (including the margins) on the desired poplar, which I cut to the exact pad size. I then layed it on the corrugated cardboard that forms the bottom of the pad.

For the white in the waves and the seagulls, I used holly veneer. I didn't have any holly the full size of the picture, so I

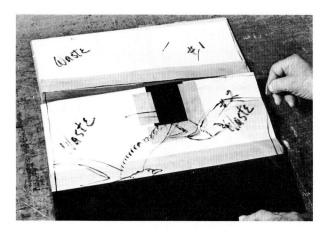

From *Fine Woodworking* magazine (Winter 1976) 5:38-40

In bottom left photograph on p. 32, the pad is being made up of good veneers and wasters, using an acetate finder to help orient the grain; right photo shows the back-lit assembly table, with a sheet of masking tape ready to take the cut pieces. On this page, right, top two photos, the author cuts the pad on his jigsaw; next, he places the pieces on the masking tape. At bottom, he uses sand heated on a hot plate to put shading on the veneer, right, and applies the tip of a gull's wing, left. The finished picture is shown at top of p. 32, with reverse side up, ready for gluing and mounting.

cut two pieces, one overlapping the waves and the other covering the birds. Since the birds reached from one end of the sky to the other, wasters would have been impractical, so I used another piece of holly, again overlapping the bottom piece. This formed the second sheet in the pad. The third veneer was a sheet of oak dyed with ferrous sulfate to a dark bluish-gray. This formed the wings. Since the seagulls occupied only about two-thirds of the picture, the veneer was cut to that size and a waster taped to it. The fourth sheet contained black-dyed veneer for parts of the waves and the water, and to it I attached a waster of maple veneer, into which I patched another piece of black veneer for the wing tip of one bird. The last sheet contained a green-dyed ash veneer, also for the waves, with a waster for the balance of the picture. All of the joined pieces in the pad were taped together with gummed craft tape to form one sheet. The pad was then ready to be taped at the edges and sawed. (The orange beaks of the birds were so small that I cut them separately and then fitted them into their proper places. The same was true of the eyes. I drilled two holes through the pad and, after the birds were assembled, inserted small pieces of black-dyed veneer.)

To assemble the cutout pieces a sheet of masking tape is made, the same size as the picture plus a margin. To do this, lay the design on a clean wooden surface, with the bottom of the design at the edge of the table. Fit a 2-foot carpenter's square around the design on the top and left side. Mark the size of the picture on the right with a pencil and remove the design. Place a piece of 2-inch masking tape, sticky side down, from the inside corner of the top of the square to the pencil mark on the right. This tape is as long as the picture, including a margin for a reinforced edge. Remove the framing square and lay down strips of masking tape below the

first one. Cut them off on the right in line with the pencil mark. Continue down to the table edge. You will have a complete sheet of tape the size of the picture. It is important to reinforce both sides with a narrow strip of masking tape to facilitate removing the sheet from the table. Starting with the upper left-hand corner, the whole sheet can be peeled up slowly. The masking tape should not overlap more than 1/8 in. between strips, to ensure visibility of the design when placed on the assembly bench, which is a square pine frame, topped with a piece of plate glass of the same size. Underneath the plate glass is a fluorescent light.

Place the second tracing of the picture onto the glass and fasten it with tape at the corners. Place the sheet of masking tape over it; it should conform exactly to the size of the tracing. It is fastened sticky side up with tape in each corner. When you turn on the light the lines of the design will show through the masking tape, which is now ready to accommodate the cutout veneer pieces.

As you cut the pieces out of the pad, lay them down on the illuminated masking tape until the complete picture is formed. Since the pieces are removable, they can be corrected if improperly placed. Throughout the assembly process you have a clear view of the picture.

Next, remove the corner tapes and lift the picture off the design. Tape 1-1/2-in. gummed craft tape over the whole picture with a minimum of overlap. Turn over the picture and pull off the masking tape strip by strip until you see the completed picture in reverse.

Prepare a glue-size of half water and half white glue and brush the exposed side of the picture with the solution just enough to dampen it. Cover the brushed side with a piece of waxed or silicone paper and lay the whole picture between several sheets of newpaper to absorb the excess moisture. If you don't have a veneer press, lay the picture between newspapers and then between two boards, and weigh them down with something heavy. At room temperature the picture will dry in about two days. Inspect the picture for open sawcuts. The glue-size should have filled most of them, but if not, any open spaces should now be filled with wood filler. I use Duratite with a little black acrylic added. I mix it with water to a paste, and apply it to the open sawcuts. Press again to ensure a flat surface; it will take only a few hours to set and dry. Then sand with a fine garnet paper to make it absolutely smooth and even. The picture is now ready to mount on a panel, frame and finish.

If you intend to sign the picture, do it after the first or second coat. Rub the spot with 000 steel wool and it will then take your signature with India ink. Or if you have a pyroelectric pen you may use that before the finish is applied.

Some of the dyed veneers I use may be made from a solution of one or two ounces of ferrous sulfate (which may be obtained in most drugstores) in a gallon of water. Maple immersed into this solution will turn various shades of gray. Philippine mahogany will turn a near black and some types of oak a deep blue. One might experiment with other types of wood. Make sure that the veneers have been immersed long enough for the solution to penetrate completely through the wood. One can check that by taking a small strip off the edge of the veneer. Wet veneers coming out of the dyeing vat must be packed between sheets of newspaper to absorb the moisture. When they are only slightly damp they should be pressed between pieces of dry paper. □

Marquetry Cutting

by Peter L. Rose

Woodworkers who have never tackled marquetry before have a variety of cutting tools and methods to choose from. Depending on one's patience and skill, some will work better than others. The aim, of course, is to have tight-fitting joints requiring no wood filler except for intentional esthetic reasons.

Basically, there are two ways of cutting veneers for marquetry—with a knife, and with a saw. The knife is good for pictures with many straight cuts and geometric designs and for cutting borders and miters. But it's difficult to cut sharp turns on the harder veneers, although there are some superior marquetarians who use a knife exclusively. Also it's difficult, if not impossible, to cut neatly through two thicknesses of veneer at a time with a knife.

The saw overcomes the disadvantages of the knife by allowing tight turns and the cutting of more than one thickness at a time. But it, too, can be difficult to handle, has limitations of size, and can run into much more expense if power equipment is chosen.

Knives to choose from

The knife most used in marquetry is the X-acto knife with a #11 blade, a blade that has an extremely sharp point. It is a comfortable knife to hold and the blade is sturdy, but frequent sharpening is required. The X-acto knife's main disadvantage is that because of the thickness of the blade, it makes a V-shaped cut, spreading the veneer apart at the top. Many marquetarians overcome this by cutting their pictures from the back using a reverse pattern. When seen from the front, the cuts will have a much tighter fit.

Another good choice is the scalpel or surgical knife, again with a #11 blade. This is a flat, slim knife that uses blades about the same thickness and sharpness as razor blades. Because the blades are thinner and sharper, the scalpel cuts the veneer more easily than the X-acto knife. However, the blades are fragile and break easily. They are usually replaced rather than sharpened.

Finally, there is the single-edge razor blade which is good only for straight cuts, as sharp turns require a much more pointed blade.

Saws to choose from

The main point to remember about saws for marquetry is that the thicker the blade, the cruder the cut and the wider the gap between pieces.

Thus the popular coping saw is definitely ruled out.

From *Fine Woodworking* magazine (Winter 1975) 1:33-36

The author uses the double-bevel-cut method on a jig saw to cut a horizontal beam. Veneer for the beam is taped underneath and is being cut simultaneously.

Fret saw cuts veneer held on a "bird's mouth." Cutting is done near the apex where there is good support. Jig would be tilted for a bevel cut.

Coping saw blades, which have pins at both ends, are too thick, but the coping saw frame cannot take the thinner but pin-less, jeweler's saw blades that do work. As a result, the most-used hand saw in marquetry is the fret saw. It has miniature clamp-like attachments for holding the pinless jeweler's blades.

The blades are five inches long and come in various sizes—No. 6/0 being the thinnest at 0.008 inches and No. 1/0 being the thickest at 0.011 inches (although there is a thicker "J" series). The No. 4/0 blade, with a thickness of 0.009 inches and a width of 0.018 inches, is a good compromise between being thin enough to produce a fine cut, but not so thin that it is always breaking. But sometimes the thinnest blade is required for extremely fine detail, and the thicker blades must be used for unusually hard woods. In any event, all the blades are quite small: they fit through the hole made by a sewing machine needle, so breakage is always a problem, and much practice is required to minimize it.

Jewelers partially overcome this by using a saw that can be adjusted to hold the shorter broken blades. These jeweler's saws can also be used for marquetry, but their limitation is in their throat size. The average fret saw has a throat of about 12 inches, meaning that a pattern 24 inches in diameter could be worked on. Jeweler's saws usually have a much smaller throat (2-1/2 inches is a popular size), but this may not be a limitation for those working on small pictures.

Whichever saw is used, a jig called a "bird's mouth" must be made or bought. It is a board with a narrow "V" (about eight inches long and three inches wide) cut in one end. When attached to the workbench, it serves as a sawing surface. The blade of the saw (with the teeth pointed down) is placed close to the vertex of the "V". The saw is moved up and down in a stationary position as the veneer is fed into the blade.

The main disadvantage with the hand-saw technique is that it takes much practice to hold the saw with one hand and move the veneer with the other so that an acccurate cut can be made on the pattern line.

This disadvantage is overcome (at considerable cost, however,) by the use of a power jig saw. For marquetarians, the main requirements in such a saw are special chucks for holding the jeweler's blades, a tilting table, and a foot switch that frees both hands. To my knowledge, only Rockwell makes a jig saw that can be adapted to take jeweler's blades. The popular Dremel saw does not adapt; neither does the Sears. Another desirable feature is tension adjustment, but if this is not available, a weaker spring can be substituted above the top clamp to help keep the blades from breaking too easily. Average throat size is usually between 16 and 24 inches.

The various cutting methods

The choice of the cutting method is partially determined by the tools available. If a power jig saw is available, then any of the four basic methods can be used; but if only a knife is available, the so-called double-cut methods are ruled out.

The single-piece method

The simplest of the methods (but the most difficult to get a perfect fit) is the single-piece method. Basically, one Xerox or carbon copy of the pattern must be made for each piece used in the pattern. The pattern (or portions of the pattern) are taped or glued to each of the selected veneers. (If glued, cut the picture from the back or in reverse; otherwise the glue will impregnate the veneer and show as blemishes in the final picture.) As each piece is cut, it is laid on a master pattern, and the pieces are held together temporarily with masking tape. The fret saw or power jig saw is recommended for this method, but a knife can also be used. The obvious

Jig saw modified for bevel marquetry cutting. Original work hold-downs are gone. Thin metal sheet with small hole for jeweler's blades to go through is glued to original top.

Veneer for house beam is taped in position to back of picture being cut by double-bevel method. Other tape is holding previously cut pieces that have been white glued.

disadvantage of the method is the difficulty in cutting exactly on the lines to insure perfect fitting joints. Since each piece is cut independently of the others, a poor fit can easily occur.

The window method

A partial way around this disadvantage is through the so-called window method. Instead of cutting all the pieces independently of each other using many copies of one pattern, and then putting them together on a master pattern, the pieces are cut consecutively from a single pattern. The pattern is traced onto the background veneer using carbon paper. The background could be one or more pieces put together. (If the pattern is taped or hinged along the top of the background veneer, it will always be in register, should additional tracings be made onto the veneer.)

Larger pieces in the pattern are cut out of the background first. As each piece is cut and removed, a veneer selected for that part is placed under the opening and moved until the grain direction and figure are in their most pleasing and natural position. The piece is then taped temporarily on the back, turned over, and marked along the edge of the opening with a sharp pencil or knife. The veneer is then removed from the back and cut on the markings. It is then permanently placed in the opening and taped in place on the back side. Each part is done in this manner until the entire picture is completely cut.

The advantage of this popular method is that each veneer can be seen in position before it is cut, and both a knife or saw can be used. But the disadvantage, as with the previous method, is that accurate fitting is difficult because the pieces still are not cut simultaneously.

The pad method

A third method, the pad method, tries to get around this disadvantage by making a single cut; that is, by cutting all the pieces at once as in a jig saw puzzle.

Several pieces of soft waste veneer at least the size of the finished picture are stacked together into a "pad," and the good veneers are interleaved among them for the cutting. To make up the pad, the good veneers are positioned on the waste veneer according to their place in the final picture and fastened with masking tape. Adjacent veneers are placed on different waste veneer layers so that there is no direct overlapping. In this way the pad is built up of alternate layers of waste and good veneers, and the assembled pad can be tightly compressed during the cutting. The top layer consists of a piece of waste veneer on which the cutting pattern is glued. The average picture may require a pad having six or so such layers.

During cutting, the pad is held together with the edges taped, stapled, or nailed. Power jig saws are recommended for this method and the blade used must be one of the thicker jeweler's blades, 1/0 or 2/0. Thinner blades would break too easily in cutting such a thick stack of veneers at one time.

This is the main disadvantage of this method: the thickness of the blade, slight as it is, prevents a tight fit. Another disadvantage is the wastage of veneers. But the main advantage is that once the pad is made up, the cutting goes quickly and the pieces all follow the same curve or contour because they are cut all at once. Ideally, if the saw blade had no thickness, the pad method would produce perfectly fitting joints.

The double-bevel-cut method

This ideal can be reached by a fourth method, the double-bevel cut, but to do this, only two pieces of veneer can be cut at a time. By cutting the pieces at an angle, the gap caused by the blade thickness can be compensated for and eliminated in the final picture. The angle of the cut depends on both the blade thickness and veneer thickness, but usually an angle of 12 to 13 degrees does the job. If the angle is too great, the veneer tends to feather; if not great enough, the pieces won't fit tightly. The best way to find the proper angle is through experimentation.

Both the power jig saw or fret saw can be used with this method, assuming the jig saw table tilts. If a fret saw is used, the bird's mouth must be tilted and possibly modified to produce the same angle cut.

To start this method, proceed in the same manner as with

Sewing needle is used to make hole along line of cut. Jeweler's saw blade will then be fed through and mounted on the jig saw for cutting out.

After the cut is made, the beam is glued in place. Because the cut was made on a bevel, the pieces are not interchangeable. Notice difference in sizes of scrap pieces.

the window method. But before cutting out any piece of the background, tape the veneer that is to replace it to the back, in position. A sewing needle the same thickness as the blade and attached to a pin vise or handle is then pushed through both veneers on the cutting line. The jeweler's blade is passed through this hole (with teeth pointed downward) and then attached to the saw. The veneer is then consistently cut either in a clockwise or counter-clockwise manner, depending on which way the saw is tilted. The direction of the cut is very important because the cut pieces are not interchangeable. Again, it's best to experiment and then follow the results consistently. When the cut is completed, the new veneer will fit exactly in the place of the discarded veneer, even if the saw blade does not stay on the pattern line. The process is then repeated for the next piece in the picture.

After years of trying the various methods, I find the double-bevel cut by far the best method to use. It's also good with either hand or powered saws, so that expense is not a factor.

Most importantly, it consistently produces tight fitting joints requiring no wood filler. That frees my efforts for the more important aspect of marquetry: creating pictures that use the grain, figure and color of the woods to produce the most artistic and pleasing effect. □

[Note: The fret saw and jeweler's blades can be obtained from Constantine, 2065 Eastchester Road, Bronx, N.Y 10461. The scalpel can be obtained from the Brookstone Co., Vose Farm Road, Peterborough, N.H. 03458.]

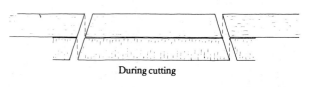

During cutting

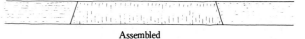

Assembled

Photograph shows "pad" of veneers ready for assembly and cutting with pad method. Cross-sectional drawing shows how beveled saw kerf eliminates gap between pieces in double-bevel-cut method.

Marquetry with Flexible Veneers

Backed material can be cut with sharp knives

by Paul L. McClure

During the past five years, I have been producing marquetry with flexible veneers. This is a perfect medium for the amateur and novice craftsman. The veneers are very thin (1/64 in.) and have a nondirectional backing blown onto them, which eliminates warping and checking. They are all flitch-matched—off the same log and in sequence. Forty species are available in flat-cut veneer, and some are also available in quartered and rift.

Since these veneers are so thin, they are easy to cut with a knife. I use the knife method exclusively. This method is not new—an Italian marquetarian, Antonio Barili, made a mar-

AUTHOR'S NOTE: Many hardwood lumber and plywood outlets carry or can get flexible-backed veneer. Constantine (2065 Eastchester Rd., Bronx, NY 10461) and Craftsman Wood Svc. (1735 W. Cortland Ct., Addison, IL 60101) sell it by mail order; stores and yards in the MacBeath, Paxton and Plywood Plastics chains carry it.

quetry self-portrait in the year 1502, using a shoulder knife. Veneers in those days were quite thick, up to 1/4 in., and he really had to lean on the knife. Today's flexible veneers are easy to cut with an X-acto knife.

My tools are an X-acto knife with pointed blade (no. 11), a metal ruler with cork back (from the stationer; it won't slip), drafting tape (it is more transparent than masking tape, and has less gum, so it won't pull wood fibers out of the veneer), latex contact cement, a brush and a maple rolling pin.

I start by finding a picture that is as close as possible to a line drawing, such as a cartoon character. The first picture I made was of Mickey Mouse, taken from a coloring book. This type of picture is ideal because all the colors are definite and require no subtle shading. As you will have guessed, I am not expert at drawing, so I try to find most of my pictures already drawn. I enlarge them by redrawing with the grid method. My

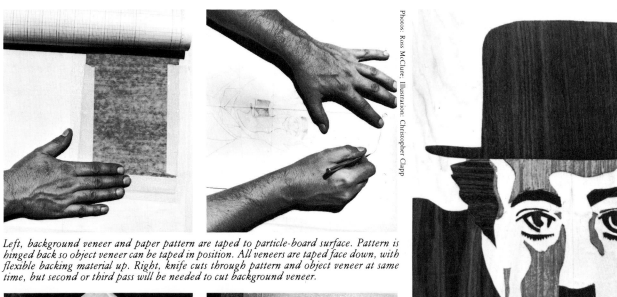

Photos: Ross McClure; Illustration: Christopher Clapp

Left, background veneer and paper pattern are taped to particle-board surface. Pattern is hinged back so object veneer can be taped in position. All veneers are taped face down, with flexible backing material up. Right, knife cuts through pattern and object veneer at same time, but second or third pass will be needed to cut background veneer.

Left, the hat veneer just fits the cutout in the background veneer. Right, with the hat taped in place from the back, the next area is ready for cutting and fitting. Scrap from the hat will make the eyebrows, hair and mustache.

Detail, 'The Little Tramp' (1977); bird's-eye maple, Brazilian rosewood, Indian rosewood, cherry, walnut, satinwood and poplar.

From *Fine Woodworking* magazine (May 1980) 22:76-77

brother is an artist, and he helps me in this respect. Creating a picture in wood from a pattern or design drawn by someone else does not prevent it from being an original—it takes creativity to obtain the desired effect using only the colors, grain patterns and textures available in wood.

Choose a veneer of appropriate color, texture and figure for the majority of the background. This is the critical choice— all the other veneers have to work with it, or contrast against it. Now choose veneers for the rest of the color scheme. Number them and their respective areas on the picture, to keep track. Also, decide which areas to cut first and which last. Remember that as you cut the pattern, it will slowly be destroyed. Normally, I start at the center of the picture and work outward, but sometimes I have to alter this approach.

On a piece of particle board 6 in. larger than the picture, cut a rectangle of background veneer 1 in. oversize on all four sides. This margin allows you to glue the completed picture onto a backing board with room to trim. Tape the background veneer face down (flexible backing up) on your cutting surface. Tape one edge of the pattern down as well, so it can be raised up and down, like a hinged box lid.

Place a piece of veneer face down under the correct part of the pattern, with its grain going in the direction you want. Make sure it's right, then hold the veneer in place and lift the pattern back. Tape the object veneer to the background veneer. Put the pattern down again, and tape its free edges so it can't shift. Now cut through the pattern and the object veneer, and try to cut deep enough to at least score the background veneer, which will leave a white line. It usually takes two and sometimes three passes.

By now, the pattern will be almost destroyed and a mass of tape will have taken its place. Pull the tape off the edges of the background veneer and turn it over. The entire marquetry surface will be revealed, and you can inspect it. You may have to make some new pieces of veneer to fit. This is done by the window method. Place the vacant area in the background veneer over the object veneer and then tape the object veneer to the background veneer and cut it to fit.

Next, cover the entire front surface of the picture with strips of tape, to hold the pieces in place and make the assembly rigid enough for gluing. Remove all the tape from the back of the picture, making sure no small bits of veneer come away with the tape, and glue the picture onto the desired surface. I usually use a ½-in. or thicker particle board or birch plywood. When using plywood, make sure the majority of the grain in the picture is going at right angles to the grain of the top ply. I use latex (water-based) contact cement. In five years, none of my work has delaminated. This type of glue goes on smoothly, does not require heavy clamping and becomes stronger with age.

Once the marquetry has been glued down, roll the entire surface with a maple rolling pin to ensure proper adhesion. Pull the tape off the veneer and you will notice wet contact cement in the joints. Sand the entire surface with 600-grit wet/dry sandpaper. The sanding dust will adhere to the wet contact cement and create a natural filler for the fine gaps between the veneers. Finish in any way you desire—oil, lacquer, shellac or plastic. □

Paul McClure, a wood technologist who has taught at the Colorado Woodworking Institute, opened a hardwood retail outlet, a branch of Wood World, in Tempe, Ariz.

Cutting Corners

How to mount marquetry

by Peter L. Rose

Many marquetarians still use white glue and a press to mount their pictures, because they aren't sure how to use the modern contact glues. And many who have advanced to contact glue use a brown-paper slip-sheet to align the picture and the board. Either way, it is very difficult to make mitered border veneers meet precisely at the corners of the mounting board. The methods described here are the least complicated and most direct solutions to these problems.

Trimming veneer

Once the marquetry picture is complete, the edges must be trimmed square and clean so the border veneers can fit tightly against them. Use a carpenter's square to mark two adjacent sides, and continue around the picture by lining up one arm of the square with one of the lines previously drawn. With a single-edge razor blade, make several passes against each edge. Do not try to cut through in one pass as this may damage the veneers.

My $30 (1977) foreign-made veneer trimmer works well on straight-grained veneers but not on irregular-grained wood. This trimmer is difficult to operate because the blade has to be set at a fixed depth; it is awkward to control when going over the veneer in several passes. Used in one pass, its cut is not perfectly straight and either splits the wood or follows the grain. This trimmer is not to be confused with a veneer saw, which works well, but for a perfectly flush cut (in matching veneers or making borders) sawn veneer must have a final sanding or planing in a wood jig.

My own veneer trimmer costs almost nothing and for me it works better. The advantage is that several passes can be made, lowering the blade a little each time by a slight hand movement. Thus it is easier to trim irregular grains and hard

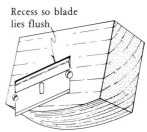

Inexpensive homemade veneer trimmer is fashioned from scrap block and single-edge razor blade, attached at an angle. Perfectly even bottom permits scoring, then successively deeper cuts. Metal straightedge can be held against back side of block, as shown here, or against razor-blade side.

Recess so blade lies flush

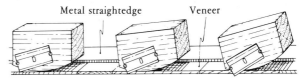

Metal straightedge · Veneer

veneer. The 3/4-in. wide block of wood keeps the blade perpendicular. Because of the curved bottom, each pass can cut more deeply. The curved bottom can be cut with a sabre saw, or on a power jigsaw with the table perfectly flat. Medium sandpaper glued or attached with double-faced tape to the bottom of a metal ruler makes a guide that will not slide on the veneer. I change blades frequently—one blade can be used twice by turning it around. Dimensions of the trimmer aren't critical, but the bottom must be even, or it will stray away from the straightedge.

Borders

Four strips of veneer should be prepared for the borders, but a good inch wider than required and several inches longer. Lay them tightly along each side of the picture, front side up, with the corners overlapping, and tape to the front. Now turn the picture over, so the back side is facing up, as in the drawing at the bottom of this column. Put two small pencil marks on each border veneer an equal distance from the picture itself, cut the mounting board to size, and align it between these marks. Pencil a line around the board on the border veneers and write "back" on the board so you can replace it exactly the same way. Remove the board, and with straightedge and single-edge razor blade cut from each corner of the picture through the corners you just penciled on the borders. Do this very carefully, as you will be going through two layers of veneer. Remove the waste and the border miters should fit exactly together. Miters cut this way will always meet exactly at the corners of the board, even if the board is not cut quite to size or is a little out of square.

Turn the picture over again, tape the entire face with masking tape butt-to-butt, and remove the tape from the back side. In a paper cup mix crack filler (sanding dust) with white glue until it is creamy and press it into any cracks with a putty knife. Remove excess filler and lay a board over the picture for several hours. When the filler is dry, the picture is ready to glue. I prefer Constantine's veneer glue because it is thinner and easier to work with than other brands of contact cement. Do not use water-based contact glues for marquetry, because the water will cause the veneers to expand, and gaps will be created in the picture.

Back

To veneer the back of the mounting board, choose a piece of veneer about an inch too large on all sides. Lay the back side of the mounting board on the veneer and pencil a line around the board. Spread contact cement thinly on both sur-

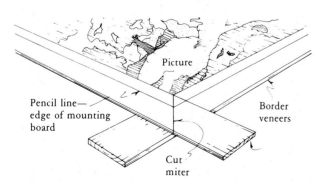

With reverse side up and oversize borders taped to picture, miters can now be cut through both borders at once to ensure perfect fit.

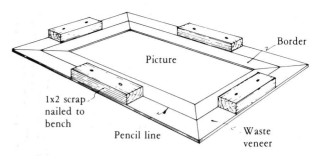

Scrap pieces nailed to waste veneer outside pencil lines form frame that aligns mounting board during glue-up with contact cement.

faces. If the wood is porous it is best to let the first coat dry and apply a second coat. Go beyond the pencil line to make sure the edges will adhere. When the glue is dry, nail four pieces of 1x2 or similar scrap wood to the veneer along the outside of the pencil lines. This creates a frame into which the mounting board can be dropped, to ensure perfect alignment. The scrap wood won't stick to the veneer because contact glue must be on both surfaces before it can make a bond.

Carefully lift the board by its edges and turn it over, glue side down. Hold it over the veneer, a fraction of an inch below the surface of the four pieces of scrap wood, and drop it squarely into place. Apply a little pressure with your hands, then remove the nails holding the scrap to the bench. Turn the board over and roll down the veneer to ensure contact. Now with your veneer saw trim off the overhanging veneer.

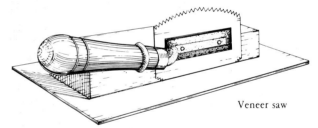

Veneer saw

Always triple-check everything before gluing, because veneers once glued cannot be moved.

Edges

The edges of the board should be veneered next. Apply glue to two opposite edges and to two oversized veneer strips. When the glue has dried (usually about 20 minutes), hold the mounting board over one of the veneers and slowly lower it into place. Roll to ensure good contact, then trim with the veneer saw. Do the opposite edge next, then the remaining two sides in the same manner.

At last the board is ready for the picture itself. Lightly sand the back side of the picture, to make sure it is smooth and free of lumps. Lay the mounting board on the picture, with the back sides of both facing up, to verify that the miters, corners and pencil marks line up properly. Mark an *X* on the top edge of the board and of the picture so there will be no guessing, apply glue to both surfaces, let it dry, and tack down the guide strips, as when veneering the back of the board. Drop the board into place, roll down tightly and trim the edges. Your picture is ready for sanding and finishing. ☐

Pete Rose is a founder of the Marquetry Society of America and writes for the Society's newsletter.

Marquetry pictures can add visual flourish to furniture of all kinds. For this walnut coffee table, Silas Kopf mounted an 18-in. by 46-in. floral picture with background of Australian laurel on a plywood base let into the table's top.

Marquetry on Furniture
Double-bevel sawing leaves no gaps

by Silas Kopf

Although we really don't have a long tradition of using marquetry in American furniture, applying assemblages of colored veneers to add visual interest to a piece is gaining favor. Veneers, sold in hundreds of colors and textures, are quite workable for making rich designs and pictures. The techniques involved, though not simple, are easily learned; the real challenge is in creating patterns complementary to the furniture being decorated.

One of the beauties of marquetry is that it requires very little equipment. Perfectly satisfactory pictures can be made with a good hand-held fretsaw or a knife, although, as I'll explain later in this article, a power scroll saw has advantages. There are several methods for making a marquetry picture. I favor a technique called the double-bevel cut, as it offers both speed and precision when making just one or a few pictures. With relative ease, many pieces of veneer can be fitted together without gaps between the parts. I mount, or press, my marquetry work onto panels, which can then be applied to small boxes and furniture of all sizes. This double-bevel method is applicable to about 95% of the work I do.

Double-bevel cutting is an additive process. You start with two pieces of veneer, one of which will fit into the other, and you build up the picture around them part by part, taping each piece into position until the picture is complete and ready for mounting. One piece is set on top of the piece it will fit into, and the saw, angled to cut a bevel, cuts through both at once. The waste is set aside and the two pieces are

placed together. The gap that is created by the sawblade is taken up by the bevel, so when the piece on top "falls into" the lower one, it will wedge in place with no space or an invisibly small space between, as in figure 1 (p. 42). The angle of the bevel is a function of the thickness of the sawblade and the thickness of the veneer. Using $\frac{1}{28}$-in. thick veneer and 2/0 jewelers' blades, the gap will be filled if you cut a bevel of around 13°.

Designing and making a picture—I try to make the picture the focus of my work and then design the furniture to best display it. This rules out mounting pictures close to the floor; eye-level application on cabinet doors or on tables seems ideal. Surfaces subjected to a lot of abrasion and wear aren't good locations for marquetry, but tabletops will hold up fine if they are protected with a hard surface finish such as polyurethane. Keep in mind that tabletops are horizontal surfaces that are frequently cluttered, so your efforts may be invisible much of the time.

Using marquetry on furniture calls for relatively large pictures that fit the human scale of pieces being decorated. A tiny, detailed rendering, for instance, goes better on a small box than in a tabletop. Attention should be paid to grain texture and figure as well, since this has a great deal to do with the size and scale of a picture. Marquetry pictures of any size are possible, and with a little planning the throat opening of the saw needn't restrict picture size—you can make

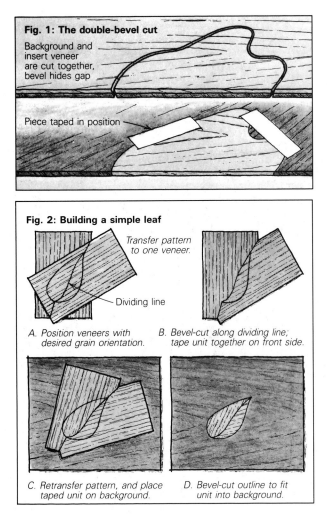

Fig. 1: The double-bevel cut

Background and insert veneer are cut together, bevel hides gap

Piece taped in position

Fig. 2: Building a simple leaf

Transfer pattern to one veneer.

Dividing line

A. Position veneers with desired grain orientation.

B. Bevel-cut along dividing line; tape unit together on front side.

C. Retransfer pattern, and place taped unit on background.

D. Bevel-cut outline to fit unit into background.

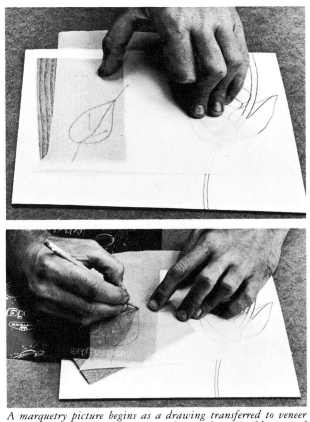

A marquetry picture begins as a drawing transferred to veneer with tracing and carbon paper. In the top photo, Kopf has traced the leaf and positioned it on the veneer for a pleasing grain orientation. Next, to transfer the pattern, he slips carbon paper between the tracing paper and the veneer. He often skips the transfer, preferring to just draw his picture directly on the veneer. This allows more spontaneity—the successful picture relies as heavily on the wood's figure as it does on a preconceived plan.

several small pictures in sections and put them together later on the finished piece.

Making the picture itself with the double-bevel technique can best be explained by using a leaf pattern consisting of two pieces of the same kind of veneer joined at the middle in the process shown in figure 2. This leaf "unit" is then placed in a background of another color of veneer. When you double-bevel cut two pieces of veneer, you may find it helpful to put a little rubber cement between the pieces to keep them from slipping during cutting. The rubber cement will have to be cleaned off before pressing, so to avoid that step, you can rely on finger pressure to keep the veneer aligned. Transfer the leaf pattern using the method described in the photos above.

To set the leaf into the picture, place it on the background and then drill a $\frac{1}{16}$-in. hole through the taped unit and the background. The hole can go anywhere on the outline of the leaf, although it's more practical to drill where another part, such as a stem, can ultimately cover the hole. Insert the sawblade through the hole and saw around the perimeter of the leaf, again on a bevel. After sawing, the leaf should fit into the background with tight joints.

As you build the picture, hold it together with veneer tape applied to what will eventually be the front or exposed part of the picture. The tape will obscure the face side, so you'll have to transfer your patterns to the back as the work progresses. This will make it possible to see the joints and align your tracings with parts that are already in place. You can

make more complex patterns by transferring then sawing more and more pieces into the package. It is always the same additive process. Occasionally multi-piece units will be added to one another, a flower for example. The individual petals each have three or four parts, which are made up separately. Then they are all added together to make the more complex flower. Experience will show where to make these divisions. Parts that are structural units, such as petals, a face or a tree, work well as single marquetry units.

The actual cutting can be done by hand or with a power scroll saw. If you do it by hand, use a deep-throat fretsaw and a V-notch bird's-mouth saw table made from scrap. With a little practice, you'll be able to hold the saw at the correct angle while manipulating the work over the bird's mouth. When cutting by hand, you should back the veneer with a waste piece to keep work from being splintered by the downward pressure of the saw. Poplar works well as a waste veneer because it saws easily and is inexpensive.

Sawing with a power scroll saw has several distinct advantages over hand-sawing. First, the bevel is maintained at a constant angle by tilting the table of the saw. Second, both hands are free to steer the wood through the sawblade. Third, the work gets better backup support from the narrow opening in the saw table, so no waste veneer is necessary for most cuts. Finally, the throat opening of the stationary saw is often larger, allowing a bigger picture to be made more conveniently. My saw has a 24-in. throat, versus the 12-in. of a deep-

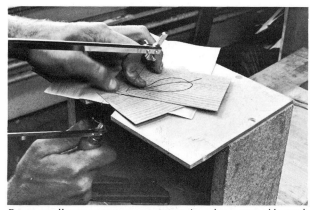

Power scroll saws ease marquetry cutting, but acceptable work can be done with a fretsaw and a bird's-mouth jig, here made of plywood nailed to a box clamped to the bench. Kopf is cutting a leaf pattern, and he is using a waste sheet of veneer as a backing to keep the saw from splintering the back side of the cut.

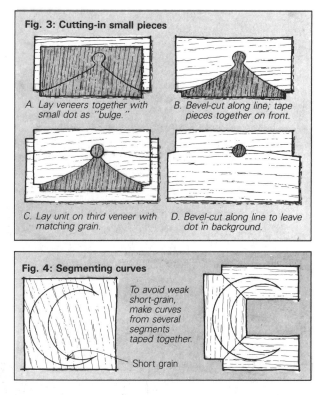

Fig. 3: Cutting-in small pieces

A. Lay veneers together with small dot as "bulge."

B. Bevel-cut along line; tape pieces together on front.

C. Lay unit on third veneer with matching grain.

D. Bevel-cut along line to leave dot in background.

Fig. 4: Segmenting curves

To avoid weak short-grain, make curves from several segments taped together.

Short grain

throat fretsaw. (See pp. 81-83 for Ken Parker's article on his marquetry-cutting jigsaw.)

I have removed the hold-down device from my saw so I can better see the saw line. The blade can easily bind in the narrow kerf, so I have to hold my fingers close to the sawblade to keep the veneer from jumping on the upstroke. This sounds dangerous but really isn't, since the saw's short strokes make it unlikely that your fingers could be dragged into the blade. Even if they are, the blade is so fine that it doesn't cause much more than a nick.

The most difficult maneuver in the double-bevel cut is the nearly complete turn around to make a pointed part. When you reach that stage in the cut, the veneers are pivoted with the saw running. While pivoting, pull back slightly so there is pressure on the rounded back of the blade and you can hear that it is not cutting. When the pieces are swung around to the proper orientation, continue cutting on the line. This will make the parts pointed and not rounded over, giving the whole picture a crisper look.

Breaking sawblades is a constant and annoying problem for the marquetarian. The choice of sawblades is a compromise between a thin sawkerf and strength. With double-bevel cutting, 2/0 blades work well. Standard jewelers' sawblades have teeth spaced closely together for cutting metal. These cause problems with certain woods, particularly when power-sawing. Resinous woods, such as rosewood, clog the teeth, overheating the blades and causing them to snap. Double-tooth (skip-tooth) blades are better for marquetry because they adequately clear away the sawdust.

When a blade does break in the middle of a perimeter cut, I return to the original drill hole to restart the cut because it is difficult to insert a new blade in the kerf. When you change the blade the unit may move, so realign it and the background veneer. Retracing a cut in the kerf is also difficult; it's best to saw the perimeter in the other direction, tilting the saw table the opposite way so the bevel will match where they meet.

It is difficult to double-bevel small pieces, but one way is to start larger and cut back. For instance, to make a ⅛-in. dot of walnut in a maple background, scribe the walnut as a "bulge," as in figure 3. Double-bevel along this line and place the completed unit on a second sheet of maple, taking care to match the grain. The next cut will bevel the two ma-

ple veneers together along the grain for an almost invisible joint, while at the same time leaving the dot in place.

Sometimes it's better to knife-in small parts, using the window method. With this method a hole is cut into the background and the piece to be let in is set underneath. You don't need a double bevel here, because the knife takes no kerf. The hole's outline is scribed with a knife, the piece removed and the cut finished. The piece is then ready to be taped in place. In cutting with the knife, only one piece is cut at a time. When you use the window method, the piece to be let in can be slid around until the grain is oriented to best tell the marquetry story.

Selecting veneer—Certain species of wood work beautifully and look good in a marquetry picture. As a general rule the softer or more closely grained the veneer, the easier it is to saw. An open-grained wood, such as oak, takes a little extra care, as it tends to splinter away, particularly in short-grain situations. A single layer of tape covering these spots before the veneer is cut will often hold the wood fibers together. I occasionally rub a little yellow glue on the surface and let it dry before cutting to help hold the wood together. Backing troublesome parts on the power saw with waste veneer also helps. Experience and a few shattered parts will, in time, identify the problem woods. Parts that do shatter can sometimes be salvaged by gluing or taping them together until they go into the picture and are eventually pressed.

As with all woodworking, you want wherever possible to avoid short grain and its inherent weakness. Thin parts will cut better if the grain is aligned with the long axis. It is often advisable to segment the pieces when forming a thin curve, as with the crescent in figure 4. Tape the segmented pieces together as you go.

At this point a word about veneer tape might be helpful. Every new piece that is cut means the addition of another

Marquetry panels are pressed onto curved tops in this particleboard jig Kopf mounts in his veneer press. The picture is laminated to a subbase of three 1/8-in. lauan plywood sheets. Scrap Masonite and a rubber sheet put between the form and the work spread clamping pressure, and bridge the jig's irregularities.

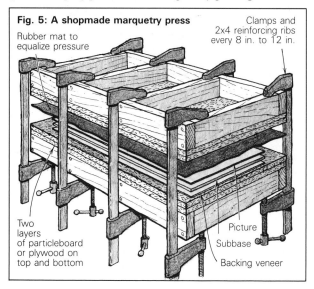

Fig. 5: A shopmade marquetry press

Rubber mat to
equalize pressure

Clamps and
2x4 reinforcing ribs
every 8 in. to 12 in.

Two
layers
of particleboard
or plywood on
top and bottom

Picture

Subbase

Backing veneer

of attaining a three-dimensional illusion in marquetry is to scorch the wood in hot sand to darken it, simulating a shadow. I have a hot plate with a cast-iron skillet heating sand whenever I'm working on a picture. The depth of the sand is about 1½ in. The deeper the veneer is shoved into the sand, the darker the scorching, because the temperature is hottest at the bottom. This yields a gradation of color that is particularly fitting for shadows. Various woods react differently to the treatment. Soft woods scorch more quickly than harder species. Pointed parts have more surface area exposed to the hot sand and therefore burn faster. Dip the piece in and out until the desired shade is reached. Sand-shaded parts should be slightly darker than you would ultimately like, as there is some surface charring that will be scraped and abraded away after the picture is pressed.

Instead of plunging the piece of veneer into the sand, it is sometimes easier to scoop the hottest sand from the bottom of the frying pan and run the wood through it. I use an old gouge for a scoop. By pulling a curved piece, such as the crescent in figure 4, through the hot sand in the scoop I can char the veneer evenly. In the skillet, the thin ends would burn before the center of the arc became dark enough. You can also stain marquetry parts before or after they are assembled, and dyed veneers of various colors and species are sold by marquetry suppliers.

Mounting or pressing—After the parts have been cut, the picture should be checked over to see if all the parts are present and accounted for. Any missing pieces can be knife-cut in. The finished picture can then be mounted to the panel or subbase that will hold it together after the tape is removed. This panel can become a decorative element in a piece of furniture or it can be put in a frame for display. In any case, a marquetry picture should have solid wood around its edges to protect the veneer from damage.

I prefer lauan plywood as a subbase. It's cheap and available and usually free of voids. I apply many of my marquetry pictures to small boxes with curved tops. (I laminate the top in a curved form from three layers of 1/8-in. plywood, glued up with alternating grain for strength and stability.) Other types and thickness of plywood and particleboard work fine as marquetry bases, but solid wood panels should be avoided. They move too much during seasonal moisture changes, and this can pop loose small veneer pieces or cause serious cracks. Subbases should get a backing veneer on the side opposite the picture to keep the panel balanced and prevent warping.

Pressing the picture onto the surface is essentially like any other veneering operation. The key in marquetry is to equalize the pressure over the entire surface. With the slight differences in thicknesses of veneers and the buildup of veneer tape in concentrated areas, the potential for uneven pressure is ever present. A veneer press is the best way to ensure even pressure. But it's a bulky and expensive piece of equipment for the occasional maker of marquetry panels. Not owning one needn't stop you from trying marquetry. Thick pieces of particleboard and quick-action clamps can make a suitable press (figure 5). To spread the pressure evenly, I use a hard rubber mat 1/16 in. thick between the picture and the press. The mat, which I bought at a rubber supply house, is similar to tire inner-tube rubber.

A variety of adhesives can be used, but I generally choose urea-formaldehyde glue. It has several advantages: it spreads

layer of tape. When there are a number of small pieces in a small area, the thickness of the tape can be a factor when the picture is pressed. The thinnest tape I have found is a 30-gram paper tape manufactured by the Ubro company in West Germany and available from Woodcraft and from Welco Machines, PO Box 18877, Memphis, Tenn. 38118. Even using the thinner tape, the buildup may be so heavy that it's best to remove all the built-up tape and then retape, so that one even layer holds all the little pieces together.

It is important to realize that the colors and contrasts you see when you choose veneer will not necessarily be there in the end. Finishing generally changes the wood color, and it is not always an even change in tone from wood to wood. Time will also alter the picture considerably. Light woods tend to darken and dark woods get lighter, giving the marquetry picture a progressively monochromatic look as time passes. This is why old work often seems faded: it is faded. These color changes are unpredictable, so I usually don't try to compensate for them in my designs.

There are tricks for manipulating color. A traditional way

Kopf applies his marquetry to furniture, but small jewelry boxes are a more frequent showcase for his art. After the picture has been mounted and let into the tops of these boxes, Kopf trims the joint between frame and picture with a contrasting wood.

easily, allows a long open time, and also fills gaps by curing to a neutral tan color (of course *you* won't have any gaps to worry about). I don't use contact cements at all because they seem to be unreliable for veneer work.

The marquetry picture should be oriented with the grain direction of the majority of its pieces running at 90° to the grain of the subbase. Run the grain of the backing veneer in the same direction as the picture. Spread glue evenly on the subbase, picture and backing veneer, and then press or clamp it up and let the assembly cure in the press for 12 hours.

The pressed picture emerges from the press covered with veneer tape and isn't much to look at. I remove most of the tape with a hand scraper, working with the grain as much as possible. Then I finish the job with sandpaper. Sometimes it's safer to forgo the scraper and sand the tape off, as pieces that are cross-grain to one another have a way of being torn out by the scraper. I use a hard cork block with 80-grit paper for the initial sanding. The flat block keeps the softer woods from abrading away faster than their harder neighbors, thus keeping the picture from becoming wavy. Because the felt bottom of an orbital sander is particularly prone to leaving a wavy surface, use one only for a final cleanup of cross-grain scratches, using 220-grit paper.

There are two repair problems that will probably occur at some time or other in your marquetry experience. The first is a "blister" in the veneer caused by improper adhesion. The blister is evidenced by a hollow sound when you rub your finger over the work. If an individual marquetry piece has not adhered, raise it with a knife, inject glue under the wood and reclamp, using cauls to localize the pressure over the repair. If the problem is in the middle of a larger expanse of background, slice the blister open along the grain with a knife, again inject glue beneath it and then reclamp the piece.

The second problem you may encounter is scraping or sanding through the veneer. The repair is made by inlaying a patch into the marquetry panel. Let's assume you have gone through at a particular spot. Select a piece of veneer, preferably from the same flitch, which has grain characteristics similar to the piece being replaced. The borders of the inlay patch should parallel the grain of the background and run from marquetry pieces inside the picture to the picture's outer edge, as above. This leaves you with a patch without end-grain butt joints, and it should be less visible. Make a tracing of the area to be recut and use the tracing as a pattern to mark and cut the patch. Bevel the cut so the piece will wedge into the panel when clamped. Set the patch on the panel and scribe around it with a knife. Use a router to cut the panel·to the depth of veneer thickness, coming within about $\frac{1}{16}$ in. or $\frac{1}{8}$ in. of the knife line. Use a chisel to remove the rest of the waste material, occasionally checking the patch for a good fit. Glue and clamp, and hopefully your picture will be like new. This method can also be used to inlay veneer into a solid piece of wood, such as a tabletop. If you do inlay, try to avoid cross-grain constructions that will later loosen during seasonal movement. □

Silas Kopf does marquetry and makes furniture in North-ampton, Mass. See more examples of his work on p. 57, and in his article "Perspective in Marquetry," on pp. 66-69. The Marquetry Society of America, P.O. Box 224, Lindenhurst, N.Y. 11757, publishes a monthly newsletter with technical information on the craft.

Finishing Marquetry
Polyurethane fills pores and cracks

by Peter L. Rose

Applying a finish to a piece of marquetry differs from finishing a solid piece of wood. A marquetry picture has different types of veneers, with different colors, thicknesses and textures all blended together. There is no single method or finish that works best for all applications. I have tried oil, latex varnish, lacquer, polymer, French polish and polyurethane varnish—my comments on them follow.

Penetrating-oil finish brings out the colors of the wood nicely, but it does not conceal pores, cracks, scratches and indentations. Closed-grain woods become shiny, while open-grain woods remain dull, causing a blotchy look.

French polish, a mixture of shellac and alcohol with a few drops of oil, results in a beautiful, lustrous finish, but applying it takes practice and patience. The surface must be flawless, having no deep scratches, indentations, cracks or gaps between veneers.

Latex varnish has no luster and does not bring out the colors of the wood. I do not recommend its use in marquetry.

Brushing lacquer, if applied correctly, will give a nice smooth finish. It cannot be brushed on like varnish, however, because it dries fast, and back-and-forth strokes will create a tacky mess. Spraying lacquer gives good results, but the equipment is expensive when marquetry is a hobby and not a business. An exhaust fan is a must because the fumes are flammable and toxic. Aerosol-spray lacquer or varnish works well with small pictures and objects.

Polymer finish is a thick, two-part mixture that is self-leveling and covers well. One coat conceals most imperfections and gives a smooth finish with little effort. Some feel it is the ideal coating, but it looks artificial to me.

Polyurethane varnish is synthetic and gives a lustrous finish without an artificial look. White woods tend to yellow slightly. While many think this is a disadvantage, I believe it gives a picture a mellow look. Of all the brands I have tried, Sears Polyurethane Plastic, Flecto Varathane and Constantine's Wood-Glo are my favorites.

After the picture has been mounted and cleaned of glue, I cradle it between four strips of wood the same thickness as the picture. The strips are nailed to the workbench flush against the picture, and keep it from moving. The next step is sharpening a hand scraper. A properly sharpened hand scraper can level different thicknesses of veneer in a short time, while sanding blocks tend to follow the contours of the surface. I use a 3-in. by 5-in. No. 0 Stanley scraper.

To flatten and smooth the picture, push the sharpened scraper at about a 75° angle with both thumbs in the center to give it a slight curve. Start at the edge of the picture and push against the predominant grains. Do not go against the grain of the border veneers. Do these separately. Be careful not to scrape through the veneers.

The next step is to apply a couple of coats of shellac. Place the picture on a few pieces of scrap wood, shimming them

Finishing marquetry begins with scraping the picture smooth and flat, then sealing it with shellac and sanding it. Four strips of wood nailed to the workbench hold the picture in place.

level if necessary, so shellac will not settle at one of the edges of the picture. Obtain a 3-lb. cut of white shellac that has a date marked on the container—the shelf life of white shellac is about six months to a year. Always buy the smallest can of shellac available—you need only a small amount. Try the shellac on a piece of scrap. It should be dry within two hours—if it isn't, it will remain gummy and should be discarded. Mix the shellac with an equal amount of denatured alcohol and apply to the picture. Let dry and apply another coat. This seals the wood and keeps the lighter woods free of the dust of darker woods when sanding. It also seals in the oil of veneers such as rosewood and teak.

After the second coat of shellac has dried, place the picture back between the four wood strips. Use a sanding block about 1 in. by 2½ in. by 4½ in. Glue a piece of felt to one side, then wrap it with a piece of 180-grit garnet paper. Or use a portable in-line sander as I do. Sand with the grain of the predominant veneers. Follow the grain on borders and edges also. Do not press too hard at the edges because the veneer will wear down quickly there. Veneers are thin so sand with care. When the surface is fairly smooth, vacuum the picture.

Now place the picture on the short pieces of wood that were used when applying shellac, or on a finishing turntable, which is easy to make and lets you see the varnish from all angles. To build one, you'll need two pieces of wood, a lazy-susan bearing and some strips of rubber. The wood for the base should be about 2 in. by 8 in. by 12 in., although size isn't critical. The bearing is sandwiched between the base and the top, which measures about 1 in. by 8 in. by 8 in. A 6-in. bearing should be used for pictures up to 14 in. by 17 in. Rubber strips (or weatherstripping with adhesive on one side) attached to the top will keep the picture from sliding as it is turned. Use strips of masking tape on the bottom of the turntable to level it on your workbench.

With a 2-in. or 3-in. varnish brush and a can of polyurethane varnish, you are ready to start. For the first several coats, don't be overly concerned about dust. Most of the varnish will be removed by sanding. Brush first with the grain, then against the grain and then again with the grain, brushing the edges last. Don't apply too heavy a coat of varnish, or you will end up with a gummy surface. The next day sand quite a bit of the varnish off the surface with 180-grit paper. The idea here is to fill the pores and cracks without

From *Fine Woodworking* magazine (November 1980) 25:90-91

Photos: James Kent Kittle; drawing: Ric Lopez

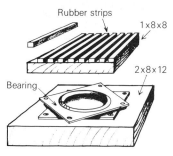

Rubber strips

1x8x8

Bearing

2x8x12

Six to twelve coats of polyurethane fill the pores and cracks (above) without varnish buildup if the surface is sanded almost down to the wood (below) with 180-grit between all but the last two coats. Placing the picture on the specially made lazy susan, drawn at left, allows you to turn and inspect the varnished surface from all angles as you work.

Before the top coats are applied, varnish, painted in with a small brush, fills deep scratches and gaps in veneer joints. The 18-in. by 20-in. picture, by the author, includes holly swans in a black beam pond under an aspen sky.

building up too much varnish. It takes about six to twelve coats to achieve this. Lightly sand the last two coats with 240-grit.

Clean the brush after each coat of polyurethane. I swish the brush around in a mixture of part lacquer thinner and part turpentine, followed by a soapy water wash and a final clear rinse. Excess water is wiped off and the brush is hung up over the hot-water heater to dry for the next day's use.

Sometimes deep scratches or gaps in veneer joints are noticed after several coats of varnish have been applied. After the varnish has dried for about four hours, use a toothpick or a fine artist's brush to fill the gaps with more varnish. They'll be sanded down the next day with the entire surface.

Before the last three or four coats, use a tack rag to clean the picture of dust. A tack rag can be made by sprinkling a piece of clean cloth with a mixture of turpentine and varnish. The back of the picture should be sealed with several coats of shellac or varnish.

After the last coat has been applied, wait at least a week for the finish to harden. You will notice dust specks on your pic-

ture—these are difficult to avoid no matter how much care you take. Remove the specks by rubbing the picture with 4/0 steel wool. Place a small amount of pumice powder in a dish and dab a damp felt pad into it. Rub the pad on the surface with the grain of the predominant veneers. Experience will tell how much to rub, but remember that too much rubbing could wear away your finish. Wipe off the pumice with a wet sponge and clean cloth, and repeat the procedure with rottenstone. Rottenstone is a fine dark powder that is messy to work with but it polishes and removes fine scratches. Finally, clean the surface and apply wax—I use Pledge.

After several months, fine raised hairlines may appear where the veneers are joined, possibly because moisture has caused the veneers to expand slightly. These lines usually disappear with a rubbing of 4/0 steel wool followed by rottenstone and water. ☐

Pete Rose, of Saddle Brook, N.J., is a founder of the Marquetry Society of America (Box 224, Lindenhurst, N.Y. 11757) and writes for their newsletter.

Patchwork Marquetry
Fancy wood, plane geometry

by Mike Peck

Some of the world's most beautiful woods are available only as veneers, and patchwork marquetry is a good way to show them off. These geometric patterns are copied from traditional American patchwork quilts, so any quilt-pattern book is a good place to look for designs. For the small tables and trays that I make, I glue patchwork marquetry to a hardwood-plywood substrate. The techniques I'll describe can be adapted to make decorative panels for many other projects as well.

The designs are created by repeating a simple geometric motif—a triangle, diamond or other polygon—called a design element. With veneers chosen for color and contrast, and variations in the grain direction, the same pattern can range from soft and subtle to flashy and colorful. The possibilities are endless.

To make my patterns, I borrow a quiltmakers' time-saving trick: in assembly-line fashion, quilters cut out the design elements in advance, and later group them together to make the pattern. Instead of stopping to cut each piece individually, I can draw from a stockpile of pre-cut, interchangeable pieces. This way, when I'm putting the design together, I can concentrate on selecting triangles for color and texture.

The design element I use in my tables is a 45° right triangle cut from 1½-in. wide strips of ⅟₂₈-in. thick veneer. You can use any type or thickness of veneer, but to minimize sanding, make sure that all the veneers in the same project are about equal in thickness. The size of your design element will determine the finished size of your pattern.

On graph paper, start by laying out your pattern to deter-

mine the total number of pieces, the overall dimensions, and how many species of veneer you'll need to get the effect you want. Next, cut the veneer into strips. To avoid this step, you can use plywood-edging veneer tape, which is sold in ¾-in. to 2-in. widths. It's available at many hardware stores, or by mail from The Woodworkers' Store (21801 Industrial Blvd., Rogers, Minn. 55374) or Constantine (2065 Eastchester Rd., Bronx, N.Y. 10461). If you want thicker or more exotic veneers, you'll have to cut your own strips. I use the tablesaw jig shown in the box on p. 50 to cut my own strips.

To cut the 45° right triangles from a strip of veneer, you'll need to make the simple masking-tape jig shown in the photo at left below, or you can duplicate the radial-arm saw jig shown on p. 50. To make the masking-tape jig, stick four 10-in. long strips of tape, one on top of the other, to a hardboard or Formica base. With a razor-sharp X-acto knife guided against a steel rule, trim one edge of the tape straight. Hold the blade perpendicular to the work surface while cutting the tape. Next, lay four 3-in. long strips of tape at a 45° angle to the first strips, and trim in similar fashion. Accuracy is critical, so use a good-quality protractor or draftsmen's triangle. Now drive two brads or small nails into the plywood base so that when the steel rule is placed against them, the rule's edge will form the third side of a 45° right triangle.

To use the jig, lay a veneer strip against the longer strip of tape, hold the knife blade perpendicular, and cut a 45° angle on the end of the strip, using the rule as a guide. Never try to cut clear through the veneer on the first pass. Instead, use light pressure on the knife and make several passes. Now flip the strip over and slide the cut end until it stops against the shorter stack of masking tape. Repeat the cut and you'll have your first triangle. Test the accuracy of your jig by cutting four triangles and forming a square with them. There should be no gaps. This is very important, since each small error will multiply itself several times over in the finished marquetry. If there are gaps near the outside of the four-piece square, as

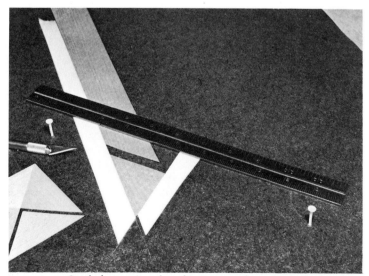

Stacked-up strips of masking tape make a simple jig for slicing 45° right triangles from a strip of veneer. The tape strips form two sides of the triangle; the steel rule, placed across the two nails, forms the third. Adjust the jig by moving the nails.

From *Fine Woodworking* magazine (July 1984) 47:62-64

The patchwork marquetry tray/table shown at left features the traditional 'Ohio Star' quilt pattern in oak, mahogany and birch veneers. To reinforce the show side of a marquetry sheet, tape along the seams of the triangles (above). Overlap the border strips at the corners to miter the veneer border (right). With a razor-sharp X-acto knife guided against a steel rule, cut through both strips at once.

shown at **A,** it means the rule is at an angle greater than 45° to the long strip of masking tape. If there are gaps near the inside of the square, as shown at **B,** the angle is less than 45°. Adjust the angle by repositioning the brads. Adjustment is easiest when the brads are as far apart as the length of your steel rule will allow.

When you've cut out enough pieces, assemble the design on a smooth, flat surface. Hold the triangles together at their corners with small pieces of masking tape. Tape only the show side of the triangles. It may be necessary to move some triangles around to distribute tiny cutting errors—it's almost impossible to make all the triangles fit perfectly. Since there is some elasticity in the veneer, small gaps can be narrowed by gently stretching the veneer to close them up.

Next, reinforce the veneer face by taping over the seams. Then flip the veneer over (taped side down) and use the knife against the steel rule to square up the edges of the sheet for the border, which can be veneer strips 2 in. to 3 in. wide, depending on your design. Flip the panel again (taped side up) and place the border strips around, overlapping the corners slightly. Hold the borders in place with masking tape and cut the miters, going through two border pieces at once. Remember to use light pressure and make several passes, cutting from the inside corner outward. Finally, tape the miters and the joint where the border meets the marquetry. At this point, your project is a flexible sheet of triangles with tape all over the good side and nothing on the backing side.

Hold the marquetry sheet up to a window or other light source and mark any gaps. Fill these with wood putty that matches the wood. Use the putty sparingly, and carefully scrape off any excess. Any putty or dirt caught between the

veneer and the substrate will cause a bump that's easy to sand through. It's a good idea to bond some veneer pieces to a scrap of plywood and test-sand them to see how easy it is to sand through the veneer. If you know what an impending sand-through looks like, you'll know when to stop sanding before it's too late.

Next, glue the marquetry sheet to the substrate, which in my pieces is furniture-grade hardwood-veneer plywood. I know that it's recommended practice to veneer both sides of a panel to eliminate warp and movement, but I buck tradition and veneer only one side. So far, I've had no problems.

Although many veneering experts advise against it, I glue down the marquetry sheet with solvent-based contact cement. It works fine if you apply two coats. I recommend Weldwood Contact Cement. Follow the label instructions faithfully, and note the safety precautions—solvent-based contact cement is extremely flammable.

With a paintbrush or a short-napped roller, apply a uniform coat of cement to both the untaped side of the marquetry and the best side of the substrate. Wrap the brush or roller in aluminum foil while you're waiting for the first coat to dry (which takes about 20 minutes). The cement is dry when a light touch leaves no fingerprint. Apply the second coat, and when that's dry, recoat any dull spots. A properly prepared surface has a uniform, glossy appearance.

Now lay the marquetry sheet taped-side-down on the bench and place ½-in. dowels on the sheet around the edges at 90° to the borders. Invert the substrate panel onto the dowels, being careful to keep the glued surfaces from touching, because once they do, further adjustment is impossible. Align the substrate with the marquetry and slowly pull out the dowels, one at a time, to lower the substrate onto the marquetry. Roll over the entire surface with a wallpaper-seam roller to ensure a good bond. The masking tape can be peeled off now, but be careful to avoid lifting the grain of the veneer with the tape. Fill any remaining gaps with

Jigs speed veneer-cutting

Because I produce lots of patchwork marquetry, I've made two jigs to mechanize the cutting. These jigs are handy for other veneer projects, too. One, shown at right, works on my tablesaw to cut strips of veneer from a large flitch. This jig can also be used for cutting thin stock that would be dangerous to rip on the tablesaw. The other, shown below, fits on my radial-arm saw and produces perfect triangles in large batches.

For power-cutting veneer, I use a 10-in., 200-tooth, thin-rim veneer cut-off blade, and I keep it very sharp. If the veneer is flat, I can cut about 15 sheets of $\frac{1}{28}$-in. veneer at once. If the veneer is wavy or warped, I wet it first, then dry it in a press before cutting.
—M.P.

The tablesaw strip-cutting jig performs two functions. With the two registration pins removed (above), you can joint the edge of an entire flitch with one pass. The jig rides against a piece of plywood to allow room for the flitch. With the pins in place (below) and the jointed edge butted against them, you can rip strips. Strip width equals the distance from the pins to the blade. To vary the width, move the pins to different holes.

Radial-arm saw jig (above and in drawing below) produces triangles in quantity.

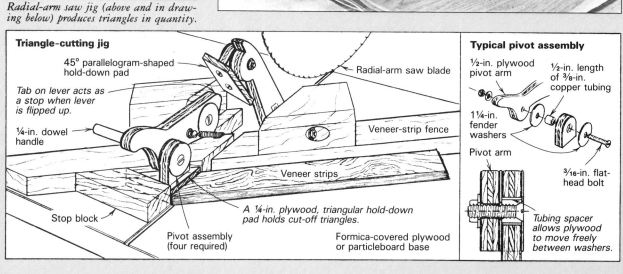

Triangle-cutting jig

45° parallelogram-shaped hold-down pad

Radial-arm saw blade

Tab on lever acts as a stop when lever is flipped up.

¼-in. dowel handle

Veneer-strip fence

Veneer strips

Stop block

A ¼-in. plywood, triangular hold-down pad holds cut-off triangles.

Pivot assembly (four required)

Formica-covered plywood or particleboard base

Typical pivot assembly

½-in. plywood pivot arm

½-in. length of ⅜-in. copper tubing

1¼-in. fender washers

Pivot arm

³⁄₁₆-in. flat-head bolt

Tubing spacer allows plywood to move freely between washers.

---

wood putty, and you're ready to finish-sand.

Before you actually begin sanding, scribble pencil lines over the marquetry. These serve as a reference to help prevent you from sanding through the veneer. Because the grain direction in patchwork marquetry runs in all directions, I just sand with an orbital sander and 220-grit garnet paper. Sand until the pencil lines are almost gone. Go slowly and inspect the surface frequently, especially if you're using thin veneers, such as plywood edging strips. Remove the last traces of pencil with

finer paper. I follow up by buffing with 0000 steel wool. A tung-oil and varnish mixture makes a nice finish, but you can use any finish you like. □

Mike Peck designs and builds furniture and hardwood gift items in Atascadero, Calif. Photos by the author. For a shooting board to help cutting straight-edged veneer for butt joints, see p. 16; for "bird's mouth" jigs to use with a fretsaw, see p. 36 and p. 43.

Marquetry Mystery

A story assembled piece by piece

by Kit Williams

When I was a boy, an old man lived near us who was a marvelous craftsman—among other things, he repaired the Queen's porcelain. He worked in practically medieval fashion and did everything by hand. "Never rely on rulers or measurements," he said. "The most important part of a job is figuring out where to begin. Decide where to put the first piece and fit everything else to it, and you'll never go wrong." I've followed his advice to this day, and it helped inspire the marquetry panels and paintings shown here, which illustrate my second book.

In my first book, *Masquerade,* the clues to the location of a jewel-encrusted hare buried somewhere in England were hidden in the book's story and paintings. Whoever put the clues together and found the hare kept it. The response was overwhelming. Not only did people try to solve the mystery, they sent me all kinds of things the book inspired them to make—I got *Masquerade* woodcarvings, jigsaw puzzles, poems, riddles, jewelry and much more. People seemed to be bursting with creativity, but needed an excuse to let it out. This gave me the idea for a second book, the title of which is hidden in its story, paintings and marquetry.

All you have to do is discover the title, then express it without using the written word—knit it, bake it, make it of wood, whatever. It's a simple title and hundreds have already gotten it right. The winning entry will be the one that delights me most. The winner will receive a mahogany box

This is the lid of the prize box Kit Williams made to contain the only titled copy of his new book. A secret compartment beneath the jeweled queen bee reveals the title.

From *Fine Woodworking* magazine (November 1984) 49:55-57

Brown oak and mahogany background veneers frame this painting. The sections making up the bee abdomens are sand-shaded.

containing the only titled copy of the book. The lid, shown on p. 51, contains a secret compartment that reveals the book's title when opened. I plan to hold an exhibition to show off all the other entries, and to publish a book of the nicest ones, many of which will be better than the prize, I'm sure.

I started doing marquetry about 15 years ago in order to frame some unusually shaped paintings. The joinery required was beyond me; marquetry, where the shape could be cut out of plywood and the veneer laid on, seemed an ideal solution. I also liked the idea of extending the painting onto the frame. I had no idea how to begin, so I bought a marquetry picture kit, discarded its picture pattern and used the veneer to make the design I wanted. I was pleased with the result, and have been doing marquetry frames ever since. I usually do the painting first, then make the frame. The story for the book developed as I did the painting and framing.

The technique I use differs from traditional marquetry, where the veneers are fretsawn according to a pattern, taped together to form the picture and laid as a sheet. This seemed too rigid to me. I want the lines to flow readily and the feeling to be more spontaneous than seems possible with a fretsaw. So I glue background veneers to a sheet of ½-in. marine plywood, using Cascamite (urea formaldehyde) glue and a small veneer press. Then I inlay the smaller pieces of the picture into the background with acetone glue (the type sold for sticking model airplanes together), which sets up quickly enough to be pressed with just a finger. My method is similar to intarsia, where pieces are inlaid into a solid-wood background, but it allows me to use various backgrounds in one picture and to avoid time-consuming excavations for the inlay.

I inlay figures like the bees on the facing page piece by piece, rather than cutting out the whole bee and pressing it

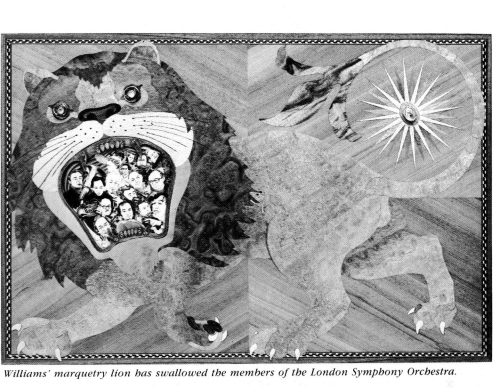

Williams' marquetry lion has swallowed the members of the London Symphony Orchestra.

into place. Excavating for the small inlays is easy. Position a piece, such as a bee head, on the background and trace around it with a surgeon's scalpel. Then score the area to be removed, push the tip of the scalpel under the scored bits and pop them out. The glue under the bits adheres to the plywood, so the inlay and thin coating of acetone glue will be even with the background. Then cut out and inlay the next piece, perhaps the bee thorax or eye, and so on.

The natural colors of the wood seem a perfect complement to the subjects of my paintings, so I don't color the woods as many traditional marquetarians do. Sometimes I'll sand-shade pieces, like the abdomens of the bees. The paintings, which are done on linen or Egyptian cotton and mounted on marine ply, rest in rabbets so they're about ⅛ in. beneath the surface of the marquetry frame. The edges of the opening are veneered, too, so you won't see the ragged plywood next to the painting. □

Kit Williams' book Masquerade *is published by Alfred A. Knopf, 201 East 50th Street, New York, New York 10022. Copyright © 1984 by Kit Williams.*

Williams often extends a painting into the marquetry frame. Here, mahogany strips outline the bird's-eye maple background veneer. The raven is made of various woods, including rosewood, walnut and walnut burl. Williams laid the background first, trimmed it with a surgeon's scalpel guided by a metal straightedge, then added the strips and the raven.

Geometric Marquetry

Terry Tallis, a sales developer for calculator products in Corvallis, Oregon, has never seen a marquetry picture that works. For seven years now, his own pieces have displayed an endless variety of wood hues, grain and texture, but in geometric or freeform patterns, never at the service of a pictorial image.

"I usually have a general mood or theme in mind, then allow the character of the wood to suggest its own design. Starting from a focal point, I select veneers on the basis of odd shadings, contrasts and three-dimensional effects. Most often I use ash, fir, mahoganies, rosewoods, ebony and birches, but I've experimented with over 70 different species, using as many as 54 different woods in one piece. Building out from the focal point of the piece, I cut the veneers individually, and match, fit and glue them directly to the base surface. Although this method may take more time and care to ensure good bonds than laying out the whole piece at once, I value the spontaneity it affords."

*Plains of Mars,
12 in. by 16 in.*

Star Plains, 16 in. by 22 in.

From *Fine Woodworking* magazine (January 1980) 20:84

Photos: Peter Krupp

James Belmonte's grand prize winner, with a picture size of only 1½ x 1½ inches, is shown here larger than its actual size.

An Eye on Marquetry in 1983
You can begin with an easy kit, but the sky's the limit

by Jim Cummins

Marquetry is a field that encompasses, comfortably, an incredible range of tastes, styles and purposes. In our culture, we can trace marquetry back directly to the time when sawing thin veneers became practical, during the Renaissance in Italy. These early marquetarians were among the first to discover the rules of perspective, and frequently outdid painters in achieving realistic three-dimensional scenes. From Italy, marquetry spread north and west, becoming an important decorative element in veneered furniture during several furniture periods. All the while, burgeoning world trade in exotic timbers added fresh colors to the palette.

Today marquetry is beginning what looks like a worldwide revival, with marquetarians in Europe having a slight head start over those in the United States. For the first time, though, marquetry is possible as a hobby rather than as an all-consuming profession. Veneers are cheap and plentiful, and the tools of the trade can be as simple as an X-acto knife or a hand-held fretsaw. Marquetry kits—a paper pattern (something like a paint-by-number design), a selection of veneers, some glue—are available by mail-order. Some kits are even pre-cut and go together as easily as a jigsaw puzzle.

Although a few European marquetarians are professionals, Americans tend to take up marquetry upon retirement, or as a convalescent pastime. Most of the dozen people who founded the Marquetry Society of America in 1972 were self-taught, and they organized not only to display their work, but

also to exchange techniques and ideas. For help, they approached Constantine's, the veneer supplier who'd sold many of them their first marquetry kit. Owner Gertrude Constantine, whose late husband had invented the pre-sawn kit a few years before, agreed to provide free space for meetings and classes in a basement workshop, and eventually, in September 1983, celebrated the addition of a second story by hosting a marquetry exhibition and competition that drew about 100 members. In 1984 the Society had about 1,200 members and had been steadily growing at the rate of about 200 per year. Past president Gene Weinberger estimated that there might be 5,000 more active marquetarians around.

There are several ways to get started in marquetry, whether you want to join the MSA or not. Pete Rose, an authority today, began by picking up a kit about 15 years ago when he accompanied his woodworking brother-in-law to Constantine's showroom. Rose says that instructions in those days were frustrating, calling for each piece of veneer to be sandwiched between two ⅛-in. thick scraps, tacked down, and sawn with a fretsaw. Rose broke a lot of blades in the beginning, but was hooked, and he soon found refinements in tools and techniques that made marquetry a lot easier. Today he writes a monthly beginners' column for the Society's newsletter.

Allan Fitchett took another route. He learned at the age of eight from an old German cabinetmaker who taught him how to inlay designs into furniture with nothing more than a

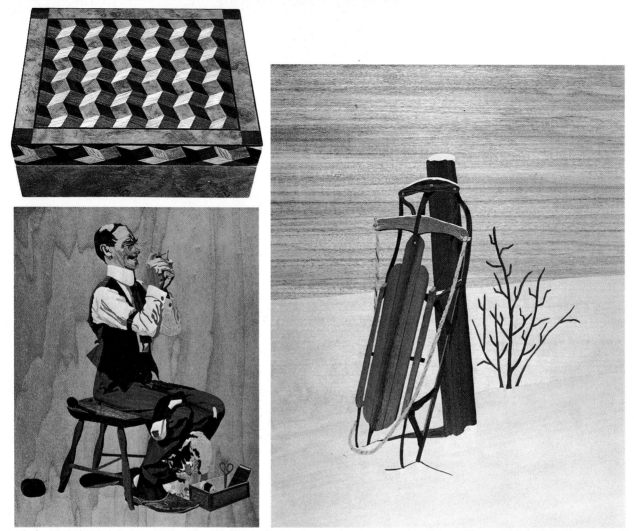

Clockwise from top left: Veneers for Meta Ketelsen's 4 x 6 parquetry box were cut on a 4-in. tablesaw. Bill Profet's 'At rest until tomorrow,' 12 x 15, won a merit award. Bill Rondholz's 'Bachelor's Plight,' 12 x 15, is adapted from a Norman Rockwell painting.

knife and chisel. Today Fitchett, a retired printer, works part-time for Constantine's as the chief of their marquetry department, which accounts for about 15% of their total sales. He gives demonstrations, lends advice, and develops new patterns for kits, such as the bluejay shown on the facing page.

Most marquetarians seem to have begun with kits, graduating later to working with patterns—the MSA newsletter always has a few—that outline the pieces but allow a free choice of the veneer. Veneer selection distinguishes the masterpieces from the also-rans. Water, sky and skin tones are particularly demanding—purists eschew dyes and stains—and marquetarians often vary a pattern to make the best use of a particularly fine piece of wood. Some marquetarians work to original patterns, but the European-professional tradition is that marquetarians work in pairs: one to do the art, the other to cut and paste. Most MSA members follow the example, with one notable exception, Silas Kopf, whose work is shown on the facing page (see articles on pp. 41-45 and 66-69). They may adapt designs from photographs or magazine illustrations, but "I'm no artist" is almost a rallying cry. This is but a minor drawback in marquetry competitions: the Society once drew up a checklist for jurying shows, and originality counted for only 10%.

The grand prize winner in the September 1983 competition, then-MSA president James Belmonte, got his waterwheel idea from a magazine ad for a woodburning kit, and spent about 45 hours cutting and finishing the minuscule picture (p. 55). He took up the hobby 11 years ago while recuperating from

heart surgery. No longer a hunter, one day he wondered why he shouldn't veneer his old gunstock (facing page). Bill Profet's sled (above), which won an award of merit, was adapted from *Yankee* magazine. Profet has an electric jigsaw, but he prefers cutting by hand, with jewelers' blades in a handsaw. So does Bill Rondholz, who adds that you can use a handsaw at the kitchen table instead of having to go to the basement. Rondholz's "Bachelor's Plight" (bottom left above), adapted from a Norman Rockwell *Saturday Evening Post* cover, hasn't a line out of place. He sent it off to a prestigious British Marquetry Society competition a few years ago, where it won awards despite an Old World tendency to classify American marquetarians as impatient upstarts. Rondholz says that it was nice to "set them back on their ears a bit." His coup was repeated at 1983's British show, where Gary Wright garnered an artistic merit award (see p. 59).

Nevertheless, Europeans still reign supreme. "Equisheim" (p. 58), by Jean-Paul Spindler, was patterned after one of his father's on-the-spot oil paintings. With a family history in marquetry, with six employees, with a "no admittance" back room guarding his trade secrets—and up to a three-year waiting list for any of his standard patterns—Spindler ranks with one or two others at the top of his profession. His work sells for up to $4,000, and he's not likely to be seriously challenged by anyone working at a kitchen table. Indeed, most of the leaders of the MSA seem to feel that such a challenge would be misdirected, that the future of marquetry lies in an

Allan Fitchett's bluejay, 6 x 8½, which he designed for a marquetry kit, requires skillful scorching of the veneer edges to produce its uncanny liveliness.

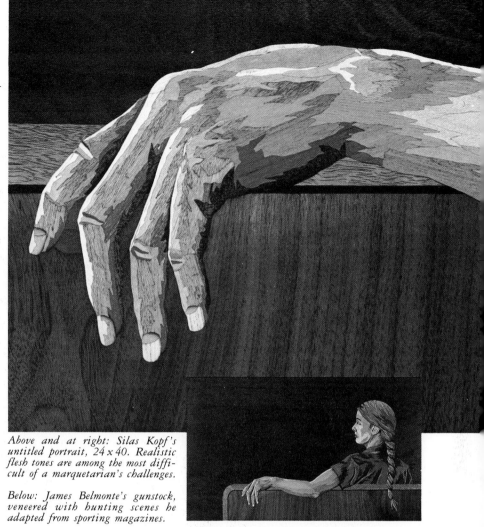

Above and at right: Silas Kopf's untitled portrait, 24 x 40. Realistic flesh tones are among the most difficult of a marquetarian's challenges.

Below: James Belmonte's gunstock, veneered with hunting scenes he adapted from sporting magazines.

Jean-Paul Spindler's 'Equisheim,' 24 x 30, is a copy of a painting done by his father.

entirely different direction, in what they call applied marquetry—inlaying elaborate designs and scenes into furniture. The practice is rare today, but it has flowered again and again throughout Europe—the Spindler family has been collecting such furniture for five generations.

"You make framed pictures for a few years and your walls will start to fall down," says Fitchett. He claims that the American character is basically impatient and productive. In contrast to European amateurs, who may take two years on a picture, most Americans aim to cut out a pattern in a dozen hours or less. Many marquetarians give most of their work away just to make room, and might welcome a collaborative effort with a period furnituremaker. The two could reproduce something more exotic than high-style Philadelphia, more exciting than just another framed design.

Parquetry, a related field, is an inlaid geometric design, exemplified by Meta Ketelsen's little box (p. 56). Ketelsen

began her hobby with a kit from Constantine's: "I didn't know what I was in for—I picked the hardest one!" But she has gone on to a rare distinction. Her original design for a windburnt sailor, "Old Salty," came out so well that Constantine's turned it into a kit and has featured it in their catalog ever since. The sailor in the kit wears a dyed-veneer sweater, but Ketelsen herself is committed to natural wood colors, and shakes her head at her single lapse, a touch of dyed blue: "I just couldn't believe in a Scandinavian sailor with brown eyes." □

Jim Cummins is an associate editor of Fine Woodworking. *You can reach the Marquetry Society of America at Box 224, Lindenhurst, N.Y. 11757. The British Marquetry Society's secretary is Mrs. Pat Aldridge, 2A, The Ridgeway, St. Albans, Herts, England AL4 9AU. Constantine's is at 2065 Eastchester Rd., Bronx, N.Y. 10461.*

Winners from the 1983 British Marquetry Show

by Ernie Ives

The BMS best-in-show winner for 1982, Richard Shellard, improved his record by taking first *and* second places in Class 5, the premier class, in 1983. British marquetarians begin in Class 1, and after four pictures move to Class 2, where they remain until they win an award, which advances them. Tony Reindorp's prize in Class 3 in 1982 moved him up a grade for the 1983 show—where he came in second against the stiffer competition—but he nevertheless recaptured the Walter Dolley Award for best picture by a non-group-member. Gary Wright's plain, bold style took the Artistic Merit Award in Class 2, the first time in a number of years that an American has won a major award in the "National." □

Ernie Ives edits the BMS's quarterly journal. Photos by the author.

Clockwise from above: Richard Shellard's 'Fruits of Nature,' 1st in Class 5; Tony Reindorp's 'Waiting for the Wind,' 18 x 20; Gary Wright's 'February Morn,' 8 x 12; Shellard's 'Threshing by Steam,' 18 x 24, 2nd in Class 5.

The intricate art of marquetry is as diverse as the craftsmen who practice it. Charles E. McElrea worked with only an X-acto knife, cutting and inlaying one piece at a time, to create "San Simeon" (left). He used myrtle burl, holly, hare wood and poplar to achieve the different colors and textures for this depiction of the architecture and landscape of one of California's major tourist attractions. The picture is 20 x 24 inches. The Moliere clock (opposite) by Charles Darg is a functional timepiece. Mahogany inlay gives this work a fascinating lustre when viewed from different angles. Howard W. Fox, who crafted "The Mushrooms" (10 x 13 inches, opposite) often executes themes from nature. In this and his other marquetry, Fox says, "I always use a piece of poison ivy — sort of a trademark." (These and the following works were among many exhibited by the Marquetry Society of America at the Metropolitan Museum of Art in New York late last year.)

Marquetry in 1975

Some thoughts on the state of the art

by Reivan Zeleznik

A quiet but vigorously intensive rediscovery of the medieval art form of marquetry has been taking place with increasing momentum. Helped by the availability of veneers of consistent quality and variety, leisure time, the challenge of working in a "new" art form, a small monetary outlay, the encouragement of professional woodcraftsmen and the cross-fertilization from other fields and occupations, marquetry now has hundreds of practitioners who have formally identified themselves with this resurgence.

Unlike Renaissance artisans who laboriously prepared their own woods, the modern marquetarian has at his disposal hundreds of combinations of species and specialties. A uniformity of thickness made possible by modern lumbering technology and the availability of supplies from worldwide sources have provided the artisan with a diversity of color, grain and figure with which he can express the subtleties of his craft. Veneers are presently available in common and exotic species. Some woods are more easily adapted to the production of veneer crotches, burls, and other distinct figures than to the lumbering of solid stock because of tree size and scarcity of particular sections.

There is comparatively little information available to describe the methods used by artisans and craftsmen of the Middle Ages. The modern marquetarian, therefore, has

From *Fine Woodworking* magazine (Spring 1976) 2:14-19

attempted to approach the art from the perspective of his own knowledge and experience, building upon and sharing these experiences with others. The availability of cutting tools (saws and knives), core material (plywood, chip core and solid stock), bonding agents (glues and cements) and finishing materials (varnishes, shellac, dyes, resins and waxes) has also increased our modern range of resources for distinctive and diverse expression.

In addition, many vocations have lent an added dimension to the art. From photography comes an awareness of composition and broad ranges of subject matter. Medicine has made available the disposable scalpel for those using the knife technique. Tool and die-makers consistently fascinate me with jigs and tools they have custom fabricated to solve particular problems encountered in their marquetry. Many dental instruments have been adapted to marquetry. The list goes on.

A retired artist who specialized in creating delicate floral stitchery patterns for fine linen and damask has adapted her talents to wood. The chemical industry has developed dyes which are now used for woods. One professional forester, Howard Fox, even injects dyes into living trees and after a number of years, lumbers them and slices his own veneers. He relies upon the trees' own transport system to spread and diffuse the dye. The result is an extremely attractive stained wood characterized by a lack of uniformity of color density.

The finished piece — a table, picture or jewelry box — represents the culmination of many laborious hours. From the conception of the idea through the design phases which adapt the strengths and beauty of the woods, to the execution which tests the technical skill of the artist, the finished product represents the love of the marquetarian for his chosen medium.

The recent (1975) exhibition at the Metropolitan Museum of Art in New York gathered a diverse and distinctive group of pieces which deserve mention, if only to describe the ranges of style, technique, subject and application.

The realism of McElrea's "San Simeon" was captured by the discriminating use of woods for the statuary, sky and architecture. Realism was balanced by Kay's "Abstract" which won the "Best in Show" award and by Parker's impressionistic "Shadows" for which he won the award "Marquetarian of the Year." Here the use of color and figure allowed few pieces to tell the story. Grain and woods were carefully chosen and were presented so effectively that to alter the choice of a single piece would have changed the mood and meaning of the work.

Highly complex pieces were equally diverse in their range

of subject treatment. For example, Morton's "The Three Months" was a skillful execution of applied marquetry that relied heavily on contrast and vibrancy of geometric design to create an exciting piece.

Op-art, dyed veneers, secular and religious paintings, whimsical adaptations of Norman Rockwell-style paintings, fragmentation, and varied cutting and finishing techniques all characterized this display, demonstrating that marquetry is now in a period of dynamic rediscovery. ☐

"Khufu" (*above left*) *by Jim Martin is a large (2 by 3-foot) impressionistic piece which will, in the craftsman's own words, "let people's imagination roam where it will instead of being locked in by any explanation that tells them what they should see." Malcolm Morton designed his 21-inch high table "The Three Months" to compliment his Louis XV furniture. The floral pattern is symbolic. Straight cutting (parquetry) was done with a taper-ground veneer blade on the table saw, marquetry cutting with a 4/0 blade on the power jig saw. The jewelry box (left) by William E. Brewerton incorporates Victorian designs and unusual woods such as koa, Brazilian rosewood, padauk and satinwood. The box stands about ten inches high. "Saint Agnes" by James Belmonte (7 x 10, left) has veneer cut into tiny bits to create a mosaic effect. Fred Hecht's "At the Easel" (20 x 25, right) attempts to reproduce the texture of cloth with walnut and maple. "Day's End" (9 x 5, middle right) by Harry E. Britton is a "wild west" adaptation of an English scene. Using only four woods, Britton evokes the intimacy and fatigue of man and horse as they trudge home after a long day on the range. Lionel Kay's 15-inch-square "Abstract" (right) was inspired by the work of the artist Frank Stella.*

Opposite: "Shadows" by Albert C. Parker. The craftsman tried to express shadows and the way they distort forms using as few woods as possible. 90 percent of this 13 x 18-inch piece is done in madrona burl and walnut burl. The simple, bold design of "Milton Avery's Woman" (11 x 17, below) by Sara Sunshine imitates the texture of cloth. Philip Fine's "Japanese Actor" (13 x 28, right) is based on an 18th-century Japanese print. Fine tried to capture the man's expression as well as the bulky appearance of his robe which is done in New Guinea wood because of its tonal quality. Lincoln B. Osborne's "Peace" (11 x 16, above) uses holly for the dove and avondire for the earth's oceans. Karl B. Zimmer's water-front scene is above right.

Perspective in Marquetry
Renaissance work inspires contemporary maker

by Silas Kopf

As a marquetarian, I often used to feel that I was working far away in time and place from the roots of my craft, which began in Italy in the Renaissance and had its major flourishing in Europe before the 17th century. I had studied as much as I could of the old work in books, yet still yearned to see the real thing. So when the chance came to tour some of the old marquetry centers in Italy, I jumped at it.

Like anyone else working with veneers today, I take my power scroll saw for granted, and I enjoy a practically infinite variety of world timbers for my palette. It came as something of a shock to see how my craft was practiced in the old days. Although the tools were primitive, the workmanship was superb and the concepts went far beyond anything I had ever attempted. The trip changed my perceptions of what marquetry could be.

I traveled through Tuscany and Umbria with Judith and Alan Tormey, two scholars who know intarsia well and also know where the best work is to be found. We started in Siena, the intarsia center in the 14th century, from which master craftsmen were sent throughout northern Italy to ply their trade. There is also fine work in Perugia, Lucca, Bologna and Florence—a city that in 1480 had a population of 150,000, yet was able to sustain 84 workshops specializing in intarsia and wood decoration.

As practiced at that time, intarsia had aspects of both inlay and marquetry. In an inlay, a hole is routed into the background and plugged with a contrasting wood. The plug is then flushed off. Marquetry yields the same look but is, in fact, a veneered overlay—thin pieces of veneer are cut and assembled as a sheet, which is then glued to a thicker backing.

One method of intarsia was like a jigsaw puzzle glued one piece at a time to a panel of poplar or pine, about ¾ in. to 1 in. thick. In the second method, the major backgound pieces were glued to the panel, and then the smaller pieces were inlaid. The portrait shown at top left on the facing page is one of a set of panels done by Antonio Barili for the cathedral in Siena. Barili used a combination of the jigsaw-puzzle and inlay techniques. Another of his panels, shown top right on the facing page, portrays an open cupboard containing the tools of his trade—bowsaw, plane, dividers, layout tools, pliers, glue pot, and a long-handled knife.

The knife was Barili's main tool for cutting pieces to shape, because the fretsaw was not invented until about 1600. At the beginning of the 15th century, the picture parts were about ¼ in. thick. By the 1500s, the craftsmen were sawing the wood thinner, yet even so, after the wood was planed and ready for the picture, it was still about ⅛ in. thick. Barili would have been able to brace the knife's long handle against his shoulder for extra leverage, but still, cutting and shaping such heavy veneer must have been a challenge, and very laborious.

The distinction between fine art and craft which many make today was unthought of in the 15th century. Intarsia was considered to be among the most important of the arts. According to Giorgio Vasari, a painter and chronicler, the intarsiatori Benedetto di Maiano achieved such renown that he was summoned to the court of the King of Hungary. "He made two chests with difficult and most splendid mastery of wood mosaic, to show to the King. So he packed his chests and sailed for Hungary." The King was anxious to see them but when he opened the parcels most of the veneers fell off, apparently because the glue had been softened by the dampness of the sea voyage. Benedetto repaired the damage, Vasari tells us, but "was disgusted with that kind of work, not being able to forget the vexation he had suffered, and gave it up, taking to carving instead."

Some of the panels have cracked and warped over the centuries, but on the whole the work I saw has held up remarkably well. I suspect that this is partly because the panels have been in churches, and therefore not subjected to the extremes of humidity found in a building with central heating. Neglect and insect damage have been much more damaging to the work than any problems with wood movement.

The intarsiatori chose their themes with care. The Renaissance interest in solid geometry paralleled the reborn interest in the Greek classics. Plato considered the five regular solids to be linked to the fundamental metaphysical elements. Writers in the Renaissance allied these forms (and mathematics as a whole) with concepts of perfection and order, representations of God. An influential book, *De Divina Proportione* (1498) by Luca Paciola, elaborated on these ideas.

Some panels were designed by famous Renaissance painters such as Botticelli and Piero della Francesca. They worked out the designs on paper and then turned them over to the intarsiatori to translate into wood. After assembling the panel, the craftsman  often added details of inlay, some pieces as small as a grain of rice and some lines as thin as 1mm. The finest intarsia pictures display a beautiful use of chiaroscuro by inserting small slivers of wood into larger shapes to create highlights or shadows through the way they are bunched together, much the same way modeling can be done in an etching by having many or few lines in a given area. The slivers will also sometimes curve to accentuate a rounded form, as shown in the drawing.

A story of one master, Fra Damiano da Bergamo, tells of an

From *Fine Woodworking* magazine (July 1985) 53:34-37

Inspired by Renaissance works such as this open-window panel by Barili (above left), Kopf responded with a whimsical cupboard with marquetry occupant.

Barili's intarsia tools seem stored away for another day's work in a panel in a church in Siena (top right). Kopf borrowed some of the master's techniques and concepts to give the illusion of a cabinet full of books, a violin and a pet chameleon.

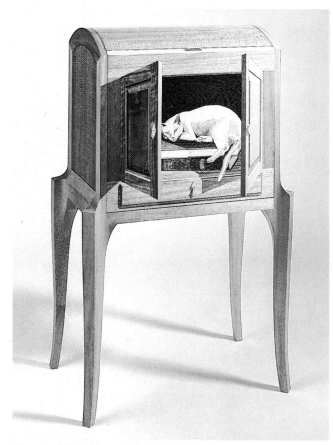

The open 'doors' and the contents of Kopf's desk are actually two-dimensional marquetry, as is the drawer, even its pull.

audience with Charles V of the Holy Roman Empire. The Emperor thought the wood in a particular picture must have been touched up with paint. Offended, Fra Damiano ran a plane over the picture, showing the Emperor that the colors and tones were not just applied to the surface. Some panels have been restored with wood fillers, but originally all the parts were wood, and they fit very tightly. Any hairline gaps were filled with earth pigments mixed with beeswax. The wood came mostly from northern Italy (tropical woods were not imported until the end of the 16th century). Nut woods and fruit woods were prevalent. These are all in the white to brown range, but the veneers could have been dyed for greater tonal variation.

There is some disagreement among scholars about how much dyeing was done. Although no one disputes that green was used (the evidence is still there to be seen), there is little remaining of other colors. There is good reason for this—most of the other colors would have faded over the centuries, or shifted in tone because of color changes in the woods they were applied to. I feel strongly that Renaissance intarsiatori took advantage of the large, varied palette available to them from the flourishing cloth-dyeing industry of the time. Wood could have been dyed much the same as cloth, using decoctions of cochineal insects for red, indigo for blue, and saffron or turmeric for bright yellow.

Marquetarians today prize veneers with bold figure and striking grain, but in the Renaissance straight-grained woods were the most common, probably because they were much easier to work with. It is only in the later intarsia that unusual grains are found. For example, Fra Damiano used burls to represent marble columns, and curly-figured wood for drapery in a door panel in

the choir of the church of San Pietro in Perugia. Visitors to such places often ask "how long did it take to make a panel?" We can make a guess. Barili contracted to make 19 panels for the cathedral in Siena. He had a nephew working with him at the time. The panels were to be completed in two years or Barili would forfeit a penalty. That works out to approximately one panel every eleven weeks per man. In fact, because of other commissions, the work was not finished for 20 years.

The strength of the classic intarsia was grounded in mathematics and the newly discovered principles of perspective geometry, whose basics are explained on the facing page. When the work did nothing more than mimic painting, it became stale. Vasari, presumably echoing (or leading) contemporary tastes, came to disdain the craft "as work requiring more patience than skill."

As for me, the challenge is still new. Before my trip, I had limited most of my marquetry to floral patterns. Now I am attempting three-dimensional illusions on furniture. Some subjects are humorous, some symbolic, but I hope that each design is harmonious with the piece of furniture and that the total concept proves provocative and interesting.

I picked up some good techniques in Italy, and I have gotten over my prior feeling that it is somehow cheating to use dyed wood—I'll use whatever I have to. In the cat cabinet shown at left, for example, the eyes and the pads of the feet are dyed. The cabinet, actually a fall-flap desk, is a mix of old and new techniques. I first made a full-size drawing in black and white, eyeballing the perspective instead of using geometry. A mathematically perfect drawing would have been accurate only from one viewing height and angle, so I tried instead to suggest the feeling of depth rather than attempt a strict portrayal of it.

Most important to the illusion are the tones of light and dark, the reason I made my working drawing in black and white rather than color. The lightness of the open door on the right thrusts it forward, as does the bright edge on the other door. Similarly, the cabinet's dark interior falls back visually from the surface plane.

With these bold areas established, I sketched the outline of the drawer and the cabinet's contents, then gave them depth by carefully plotting the contours of the shadow lines. Until I had seen the work of the old masters, I had never guessed how important shadows are to defining contours and shapes.

I had also not realized how important it was to overlap objects in the picture to help suggest depth. As I worked on the drawing, I took every chance to do so. One book overlaps the other, the cat's back leg overlaps both books, and the tip of the tail continues out over the drawerfront.

When the drawing was complete, I transferred it to various veneers with carbon paper, taking care to follow the lightness and darkness of the drawing so that the cabinet would look like one sort of wood exposed to various degrees of light intensity. I then cut the straight lines with a knife and the curved forms with the double-bevel technique. I taped the pieces together into a full-picture sheet and veneered it onto medium-density fiberboard, and then inlaid the fine details, such as the title of the book and the cat's whiskers. Studying the finished picture, I realized that the books did not stand out as well as they should, so I also inlaid a fine shadow line around their covers.

As a final touch, I inlaid the shadow of the left-hand door onto the solid-wood post of the leg. Barili, I hope, would have approved of his new apprentice's efforts. ☐

Silas Kopf is a professional marquetarian in Northampton, Mass. He wrote about veneer-cutting techniques on pp. 41-45.

Basic rules of perspective

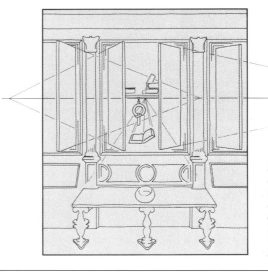

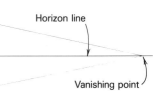
Horizon line

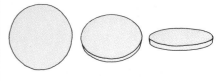
Vanishing point

Perspective drawing, whose basics are explained below, conveys the illusion of three dimensions. The photo shows a wall in a 15th-century room (now in the Metropolitan Museum in New York for restoration) from the Ducal palace in Gubbio.

As shown in the drawing below, a picture contains a *horizon line,* always at "sea level" whether sea level is visible in the picture or not—in interior scenes, for example, it usually is not. The horizon line is always at the eye level of the observer. If the picture contains people the same height as the observer, the horizon line is at their eye level, too, provided that the land is flat. The farther away people and other objects are, the smaller they look.

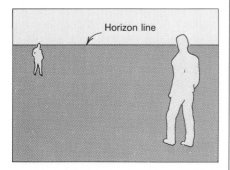
Horizon line

Parallel lines appear to get closer together with distance, until they meet at a *vanishing point,* as shown below. If the lines are also parallel to the earth's surface, they will converge on the horizon line or its extension outside the picture.

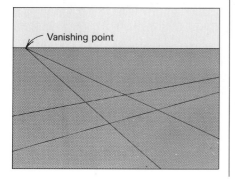
Vanishing point

Planes, such as the sides of a box, converge to the same vanishing points as the box's top and bottom. In conventional drawing, planes perpendicular to the earth are drawn perpendicular, as in the drawing of the box, below. This assumes that the observer is looking straight ahead. Exceptions occur in unusual circumstances or for exaggeration, such as when looking up at a tall skyscraper—its sides would be drawn converging.

Verticals are drawn perpendicular.

The plane of an open box lid is neither parallel to the earth nor perpendicular, hence its vanishing point is not on the horizon line. It may be above the line or below it, depending on the hinge location.

Lid's vanishing point is on a line perpendicular to vanishing point on the horizon line.

Circles in perspective are seen as ellipses. The more the circle is turned, the narrower the ellipse becomes.

The axis of a cylinder laid on its side is in a direct line with the minor axis of the ellipse representing its top. The cylinder's sides converge to a point along the axis.

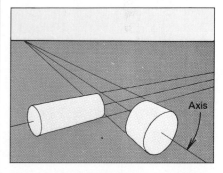
Axis

Many of the laws of geometry are still true in perspective drawings. For example, the center of a circle can be found at the intersection of the diagonals of a square drawn around it. The center of a circle in perspective can be found the same way: Draw a square in perspective around the ellipse and then connect the corners.

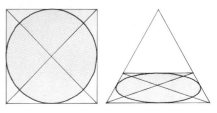

How Inlay is Made

Commercial techniques for marquetry inserts and banding

by Rick Mastelli

Traditional designs for marquetry inserts include fans, sunbursts, shells, urns, American eagles and floral patterns. They are often round or oval in perimeter, bordered by a thin strip bent around and joined, or by a thin ring cut whole from a sheet of veneer. Within the border can be any number of individually sawn pieces set into a figured background veneer of the same standard thickness. The pieces are often shaded by scorching in hot sand to give the picture the illusion of depth. Once assembled, the marquetry insert can become part of a veneered surface or be let into the solid surface of a box or piece of furniture by routing a recess slightly shallower than the thickness of the insert (for how to do this, see "Routing for Inlays," pp. 74-75). The other sort of commercially available inlay is banding, used to decorate the borders of drawers, doors, panels and tabletops. Also $\frac{1}{20}$ in.

to $\frac{1}{28}$ in. thick, it's typically patterned in repetitive geometric shapes and sold in 36-in. lengths of various widths.

There used to be many manufacturers of banding and marquetry inserts, but few survived the Depression and War years. Now there are only Danker Marquetry in Traverse City, Mich., Inlaid Woodcraft in Kirkland, Ill., Dover Inlay in Mineola, N.Y., and Jason French in West Chelmsford, Mass. Together these four supply the period-furniture industry, the mail-order woodworking supply houses, the individual craftsman, and the reproduction and restoration specialists with traditional and custom-made inlay. I visited Jason French and Dover Inlay, and I discovered that both shops make inlay today pretty much the same way it's been made for more than a hundred years. They still use a perforated paper master to make multiple pounce patterns, which they cut into the individual elements of each design. They glue these pattern elements to stacks of up to 30 veneers, and jigsaw the whole stack at once. The pieces that require shading are scorched in frying pans of hot sand, and the inserts are assembled by hand, one at a time. There's nothing sophisticated about the equipment (except at Inlaid Woodcraft, which has recently introduced a woodcutting laser). Inlay still comes from an artistic eye and a patient hand. These firms have the experience and the panache to execute traditional designs in quantity, but their methods are straightforward—you can apply them to any sort of design, in any quantity.

Jason French, 63, has done marquetry since he was a boy. His father, upon graduating from high school, went to New York City to learn cabinetmaking, whereupon he discovered inlay. He returned to Cambridge, Mass., in 1905 and opened his own shop, soon specializing in inlay. Jason has been a watchmaker and modelmaker, but he always worked nights and weekends in his father's shop. In 1968, Jason took over the business; he's not been without work since. He works with his wife, Violet, who does most of the assembly and the shading, while he designs and saws. It's very much a cottage industry on the second floor of their backyard garage. Their simple machinery consists of a Rockwell jigsaw, a Powermatic 10-in. table saw (fit with a thin-rim veneer blade), a Delta drill press and a Craftsman 12-in. bandsaw. French's pride is a 4-ft. by 13-in., 5-screw veneer press, and the thousands of feet of various woods he has squirreled away, "everything from aspen to zebrawood," he tells me.

Dover is a larger operation, though it is also a couple of generations old (established in 1919) and still works in traditional ways. It's owned and operated by Paul and Don Boege, father and son. They've experimented with various alternatives to jigsawing, the most skill-demanding part of making inlay, but die cutting, they found, leaves a beveled edge on the parts, visible as a gap in the finished design, and the laser wasn't cost-effective for the scale of their operation. They employ three people on jigsaws, including Don Boege, and at

Marquetry inserts at Dover Inlay like the sunburst, top, are assembled on a light-tack tape. Above, an American eagle in all its parts.

From *Fine Woodworking* magazine (March 1981) 27:46-49

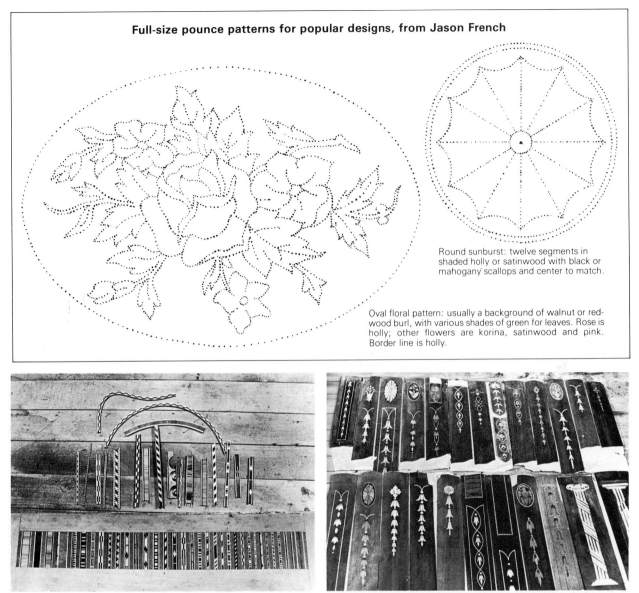

Full-size pounce patterns for popular designs, from Jason French

Round sunburst: twelve segments in shaded holly or satinwood with black or mahogany scallops and center to match.

Oval floral pattern: usually a background of walnut or redwood burl, with various shades of green for leaves. Rose is holly; other flowers are korina, satinwood and pink. Border line is holly.

Jason French's work includes banding, left, and face veneers for square-tapered legs, right. Note that these are samples and that the leg veneers would run the entire length of the leg, including the border line, which is sawn.

least four people at the assembly bench. One-third of their 6,000-sq. ft. shop is devoted to storage, mainly ⅟₂₈-in. veneers, though there's also lumber for making into banding. Their machinery is only slightly more sophisticated than French's. Table-saw tops hinge up so blades can be changed without affecting arbor or fence adjustments, and their jigsaws are large, wooden-frame designs able to cut accurately a stack of 30 veneers at a time. The saws incorporate a clutch that saves turning off and on the motor to thread the blade through drilled holes for interior cuts. One jigsaw (shown on the next page) has an almost infinite throat, limited only by the walls of the shop, for instead of an arm from the base supporting the upper end of the blade, a post mounted and guyed to the ceiling extends down to within 12 in. of the table top. The blade, powered from below, is attached at its upper end to a spring in the post. They use this saw for cutting out bell flowers and borders in face veneers for square-tapered legs and other large assemblages.

At both the French and Dover shops, a marquetry insert begins with a pattern drawn on thin, 100% rag paper from which copies must be made; the number of copies depends on the intricacy of the design (adjacent parts require separate patterns cut from separate copies) and on the number of stacks of veneer to be sawn. The pattern must realistically anticipate the fineness and curvature of the cut their saws and sawyers can manage, and notations on it indicate what kind of wood each piece will be. This is a pre-zerox method that has the advantage of a durable master from which thousands of exact copies can be made (photocopies are usually a slightly different size from the original). If the pattern is symmetrical, the paper is folded and only half the pattern is drawn. Then the paper is perforated along the pattern lines with tiny holes, spaced as close together as possible. French uses a pin and pin vise, backing the paper with an even-grained, medium-density hardwood. Dover uses a fine needle stuck in a wooden handle. To make a copy, the perforated master is placed on the copy paper, and pounce, a fine asphaltum powder (French uses pulverized gilsonite from the American Gilsonite Co., 1150 Kennecott Bldg., 10 E. South Temple St., Salt Lake City, Utah 84133) is daubed up with a felt pad and

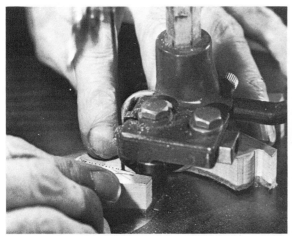

Jason French saws a sandwich of 16 veneers for fan inlay parts. The dotted line is pounce, a powdered asphaltum applied through perforations in the master pattern.

Left and above, Don Boege saws a bell-flower pattern in a stack of 30 face veneers for square-tapered legs. The jigsaw has an almost limitless throat because the top of the blade is attached to a spring in the ceiling-suspended post.

rubbed through the perforations. The copy is then carefully moved over a heating element (French uses an electric hot plate), which fixes the powder to the paper so it can't smear or blow off. The copy is then scissored into its individual parts, well outside the dotted line, and the parts are sorted according to what species of wood each will be sawn from.

French saws from 6 to 20 units at a time, depending on the run he is producing and on the delicacy of the cut—details will be cleaner from a smaller stack. He sandwiches the veneers between two pieces of plywood (¼-in. on top, ⅛-in. on the bottom) to prevent tear-out. The sandwich has to accommodate all the parts of the pattern to be cut from that type of wood. French hide-glues the pattern parts to the top of the sandwich and holds it together by driving brads through the waste areas, clinching them on the bottom side. Sawing is then a matter of care and skill. French tries to split the dotted line on both the individual parts and the background veneer to produce a good, snug fit. For most cuts he uses a Trojan #2 coarse blade, 0.085 in. by 0.020 in., 15 teeth per inch. "It says it's filed and set when you get it," he says, "but you can't believe that. I sharpen each blade before I use it, filing straight across. It takes me about two days to saw out all the pieces for a complex pattern in a run of 30, my usual number. The hardest cut in the book, though, is a long, straight line into a square corner, like on table legs."

Pieces that need shading are brought over to a sand-filled

frying pan on an electric hot plate. The pieces are held in handmade wooden tweezers, two at a time, show-face out, and dipped into the sand for scorching. The edge is made darkest, fading gradually toward the interior.

The piles of identical parts are then organized on the assembly bench around a sheet of newspaper. First the background veneer is tacked down with brads, show-face up. Then the point of a razor-knife spears each tiny piece, and a dab of hot hide glue on the newspaper holds it in place in the background. It's like assembling a jigsaw puzzle, tack-gluing each piece as the puzzle proceeds. When all the pieces are in place, French coats a piece of heavy brown paper with hide glue and lays it over the top. He presses the assemblages immediately with a wool rug for about an hour to make up for any unevenness. When the glue has set, the newspaper (under) side of each picture is moistened and scraped clean. A mixture of hide glue, water and mahogany dust is rubbed into the spaces between the pieces and into the sawn lines that represent detailing on the larger pieces. French uses the edge of a Teflon block to squeegee off the excess filler. The remainder is left to set while the pictures are kept flat under a heavy board. A finished insert will retail for anywhere from $2.50 to $20 (1981). If he did little else, French figures he could produce 50 to 75 inserts in a week.

Dover Inlay can produce hundreds. Besides its larger staff, the firm has streamlined assembly by using, instead of hot hide glue, two kinds of tape. Individual pieces are still speared, show-face up, and positioned with the point of a razor-knife, but instead of newspaper and glue, a ground of light-tack tape holds them in place. When assembly is complete, a gummed tape, similar to packaging tape, is placed over the show-face. The light-tack tape is removed from the back and a filler of water-soluble glue, water and mahogany dust is pressed in. With this method you don't have to tend the glue pot or contend with the wood curling from moisture taken on from the backing glue, and you don't have to clamp.

Banding is made entirely differently. Instead of tiny pieces assembled into finished units one at a time, a 36-in. long, 6-in. or 8-in. wide "trunk" pattern is assembled, and 1/28-in. strips are cut from it on the table saw, like slicing pastrami. Often what appears in the finished banding as tiny components is the result of an earlier generation of assembling and slicing larger pieces of wood or sheets of veneer. A typical design will begin with two or three pieces of contrasting veneer, 36 in. by 6 in., laid down with glue between. French prefers traditional hot hide glue because of its long assembly time; hot cauls applied to the assembly before it goes in the press reliquefy the glue. Dover Inlay uses Cascamite, and Danker Marquetry, the other large producer of banding, has switched to a slow-set Titebond. Next a series of 6-in. long sticks of complementary section, or a series of 6-in. long assemblages from an earlier gluing and slicing (parallelograms, say, from 45° cuts) are glued together and onto the veneer. Another two or three layers of veneer on top complete the sandwich, and the whole thing goes in the press for a day. When the assemblage is removed and sliced, the components will appear as arrowhead banding, bordered by thin lines, as in the drawing at right. With a veneer blade producing a 1/32-in. kerf, about ninety 36-in. long strips can be gotten from a 6-in. wide lamination. These sell for anywhere from $.70 to $7 a yard. Hundreds of patterns are currently produced. "There's no end to inlay," says French, "because there's always someone coming up with some new challenge."

Both French and Dover found that demand for their products increased in the last two years (1979-80). This popularity seems to be part of a cycle that has gone on for as long as woodworking itself. Interest in decorating furniture alternates with the primary interest in constructing it. Medieval joiners, for instance, when they had satisfied the demands of their time for building in solid wood, devoted more and more of their energies to decoration. Carved designs—chip carving or relief carving of geometric, floral, animal, religious and other motifs—were the most popular, but straight-walled recesses were also cut into solid wood surfaces, using a shoulder knife, and thin pieces of wood let in to describe floral patterns and religious pictures. This was the beginning of marquetry in the West. In some monastic orders, marquetry became an art in its own right, not wed to furniture as decoration, and wooden pictures came to rival oil paintings for their detail and realism. The invention of the fretsaw in 1562 took marquetry out of the domain of the artist and gave it over to the craftsman, who could follow designs prepared by more artistic hands than his own. The result was a decline in the quality of the pictorial images and an increase in their use as decoration. Throughout the ensuing era of the cabinetmaker, there can be traced an ebb and flow in the taste for decorating furniture with thin wood. At least part of the reason lies with the makers themselves. Newly challenged by the construc-

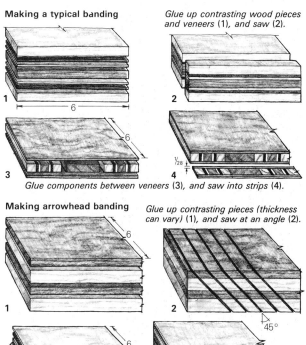

Making a typical banding

Glue up contrasting wood pieces and veneers (1), and saw (2).

Glue components between veneers (3), and saw into strips (4).

Making arrowhead banding

Glue up contrasting pieces (thickness can vary) (1), and saw at an angle (2).

Glue components between veneers (3), and saw into strips (4).

tional demands of a compound-curved surface, say, or a tambour door, the cabinetmaker is absorbed. After mastering the difficulties, he looks for more; he decorates, often by inlaying.

Contemporary woodworking seems not immune to this cycle. Since the end of World War II, when Danish designs became aligned with modern tastes, many people have appreciated solid, unembellished wood, and have been absorbed in constructing with it. Even in the period-furniture trade, Queen Anne and Chippendale have been far more popular than decoratively veneered Hepplewhite, Sheraton and Louis XV or XVI. Until recently, that is. Period-furniture manufacturers are now responding to increased interest in Federal furniture, typically decorated with banding and marquetry inserts. The mail-order companies that sell inlays (Constantine, 2065 Eastchester Rd., Bronx, N.Y. 10461; Craftsman, 1735 West Cortland Ct., Addison, Ill. 60101; and The Woodworkers' Store, 21801 Industrial Blvd., Rogers, Minn. 55374) are selling more these days. And recent gallery shows have included more inlaid work, reflecting the greater sophistication of contemporary woodworkers who have been in the trade long enough to have outgrown their image as the first wave of a resurgence in crafts. □

EDITOR'S NOTE: The Marquetry Society of America (see p. 55 for more on the Society) publishes a monthly newsletter. Write them at PO Box 224, Lindenhurst, N.Y. 11757, for more information. Books on the subject include *The Art and Practice of Marquetry*, by William Alexander Lincoln (London: Thames and Hudson, 1971); *Modern Marquetry Handbook*, edited by Harry Hobbs and Alan Fitchett (New York: Constantine, 1978); and *Veneering Simplified*, by Harry Hobbs (New York: Constantine, 1978). Write Constantine, 2065 Eastchester Rd., Bronx, N.Y. 10461, for prices and availability of all three books, or check your library for these and other titles.

Routing for Inlays
Template guides match inlay and recess

by Eric Schramm

Inlaying is often regarded as a difficult process requiring a great deal of skill. However, with a portable electric router and a fence, thin strips of contrasting wood can easily be inlaid to form the border on tabletops, drawer fronts, cabinet doors and straight-tapered legs. With suitable template guides, or with just a steady hand, the router can inlay marquetry inserts and pieces of burl, butt or crotch veneer. Inlays enhance the beauty as well as the intrinsic value of pieces of furniture, serving trays and jewelry boxes.

To cut a straight groove for an inlaid border strip, insert a straight bit of the proper diameter in the router and adjust it to a depth slightly less than the thickness of the strip. Fasten the fence at the desired distance (or if your router is not

To inlay a border of contrasting wood, rout groove using straight bit and fence. Take care not to overshoot. Square corners of groove and miter inlay strips with a chisel or knife; glue, and press in with a hammer.

To freehand rout a recess for a marquetry insert, first trim insert of background veneer, and use it as pattern to scribe outline onto ground stock. Centerlines and X's assure proper positioning. Rout to within 1/16 in. of outline and clean edge with gouges. Glue insert in place and clamp, using wax paper between insert and clamping block.

equipped with a fence, clamp a straight piece of wood to the base), and hold it against the edge of the piece to be bordered. Rout counterclockwise around the work, opposite to the rotation of the bit, to keep the fence pressed against the edge. With a sharp knife or chisel, square the corners of the groove and miter the inlay strips to the correct length. Brush the strips with glue and force them into the grooves by running the face of a hammer along their length, pressing carefully so as not to damage the wood. When dry, scrape the surface flush and clean off excess glue. Then sand and finish.

There are two methods for inlaying a marquetry insert, one freehand and one involving the use of a template. As received from the distributor, these inserts are glued to a piece of brown paper and set in the center of a piece of veneer, which protects their delicate edges. The background veneer should be removed to the outline of the insert. First cut with the band saw to about 1/4 in. from the insert itself, then remove the remainder with a sharp knife, chisel or gouge. If bits of the paper backing project around the edges of the insert, file or sand lightly. Place the insert face down on the surface where it is to be inlaid. Draw two centerlines crossing each other at right angles on the project and on the insert, and position the insert so the centerlines coincide. Trace its outline on the surface with a hard, sharp pencil or with a scriber. Before removing the insert, mark it and the surface with an *X* so they can be realigned. Set up the router with a 1/4-in. straight bit, and remove wood to the proper depth, usually a little less than the standard veneer thickness of 1/28 in., cutting to within 1/16 in. of the line. Now use various carving gouges of the proper curvature to remove the thin line of wood that remains after routing. Apply glue to the recess, press the inlay into it with the brown paper backing facing up and the *X*'s corresponding, and force out the surplus glue by rubbing the head of a hammer over the surface. Use one or two pieces of masking tape to be sure the insert stays in position. Then cover with a piece of wax paper so glue will not adhere to the clamping block, lay down a block of wood close to the size of the insert, and clamp overnight. After the glue has dried, hand-sand with 60-grit to remove the paper backing, then fine-sand the entire surface to 150-grit.

Another method of routing in inserts is to use a template. This procedure requires a 1/2-in. and a 1-in. outside-diameter template guide, and a 1/4-in. straight bit. The idea is to use the smaller template guide to cut an opening in a piece of plywood larger than the insert to be inlaid, and then to use this oversize template with the larger template guide to cut a recess the exact size of the insert. Only Rockwell makes

EDITOR'S NOTE: You can purchase marquetry inserts from Constantine, 2065 Eastchester Rd., Bronx, N.Y. 10461; Woodcraft Supply Corp., 41 Atlantic Ave., Box 4000, Woburn, Mass. 01888; The Woodworkers' Store, 21801 Industrial Blvd., Rogers, Minn. 55374; and Craftsman, 1735 West Cortland Ct., Addison, Ill. 60101.

From *Fine Woodworking* magazine (July 1979) 17:68-69

Photos: Robert Schramm

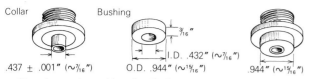

Collar   Bushing

.437 ± .001" (~7/16")   I.D. .432" (~7/16")   O.D. .944" (~15/16")   3/16"   .944" (~15/16")

To make template guide collars for Stanley routers, use two standard 7/16-in. Stanley template collars, and machine a bushing, as shown above, to press fit on to one of the collars. Individual routers will vary in tolerance, so test cut the template and recess. If the inlay fits too tightly, use emery cloth to remove one or two thousandths of an inch from the outside diameter of the bushing. If the inlay is loose, remove one or two thousandths of an inch from the 7/16-in. collar used to cut the template.

template guides of the correct diameter, but Stanley template guides can be refashioned to work. In order to use a ¼-in. thick template, as will be done here, the length of the guides must be machined to ³/₁₆ in.

The first step in making the template is to make a pattern the exact size and shape of the insert to be inlaid. On a piece of ¼-in. hardboard or solid-core plywood, scribe the outline of the insert, bandsaw, then sand to split the line. Draw a horizontal and a vertical centerline on this pattern and also on a piece of hardboard or plywood 4 in. to 5 in. larger all around than the pattern. Secure the pattern in the center of this larger piece with wire brads. Set up the router with a ¼-in. straight bit and attach the ½-in. template guide to the router base. Adjust the router so the bit projects just enough to cut through the template stock. Fasten the pattern and template stock on another piece of plywood so that when the router cuts through, it will not damage the workbench. With the router running, lower the bit into the template stock, being careful to keep the edge of the template guide touching the pattern. Move in a counterclockwise direction, guiding against the pattern, to cut out the template.

Now position the template on the ground stock to be inlaid, aligning the centerlines. Replace the ½-in. template guide with the 1-in. guide, and adjust the depth of the cut to a little less than the thickness of the insert. Again with the router running, lower the base onto the template so the template guide will run on the inside edge of the template. Rout around the template (in a clockwise direction because now the fence is on the opposite side) to cut the outline of the inlay, then run the router back and forth within the template opening to remove the waste. Be careful to keep the router base resting on the template at all times. If the inlay is so large that the recess cannot be cleaned out with the router resting on the template, remove the template and place the router over the recess on two equally thick parallel strips of wood. Reset the depth of cut to the thickness of the strips plus the inlay, and remove the remaining material. Clean out the recess with a chisel, and glue the inlay as before.

An advantage of this method of inlaying is that inlays of burl, crotch or contrasting veneer can be made with the same template. Draw centerlines on the veneer to be inlaid so that the template can be lined up. Hold the template to the veneer with brads into the waste part of the veneer. Then with the ½-in. template guide, and the ¼-in. straight bit set to the proper depth, carefully lower the router so that the guide rests against the inside edge of the template. Guide the router around the template until the inlay is cut out.

Inlaying with a template

1. Making template

Secure pattern from marquetry insert to ¼-in. plywood and rout template with ¼-in. straight bit and ½-in. template guide. Note that this setup cuts template opening ¾ in. larger than pattern: ³/₈-in. margin on each edge.

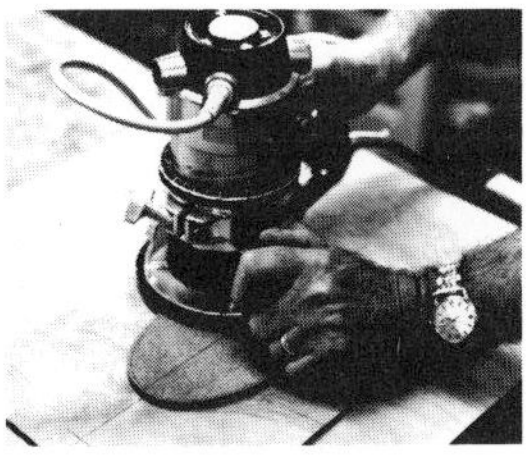

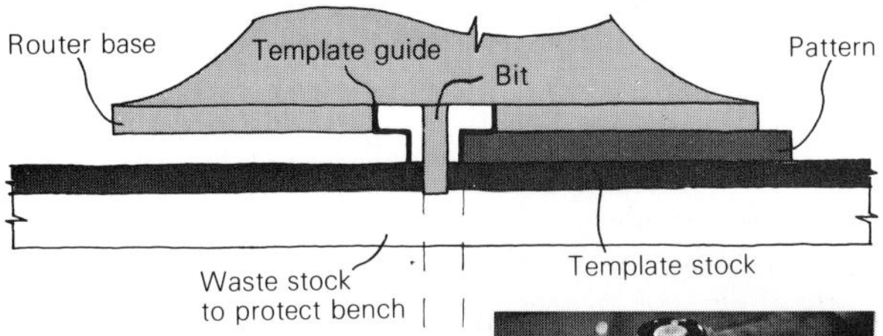

Router base   Template guide   Bit   Pattern

Waste stock to protect bench   Template stock

2. Cutting recess

Change to 1-in. guide, reset depth and follow template. Note that this setup establishes ³/₈-in. margin and cuts recess same size as original pattern.

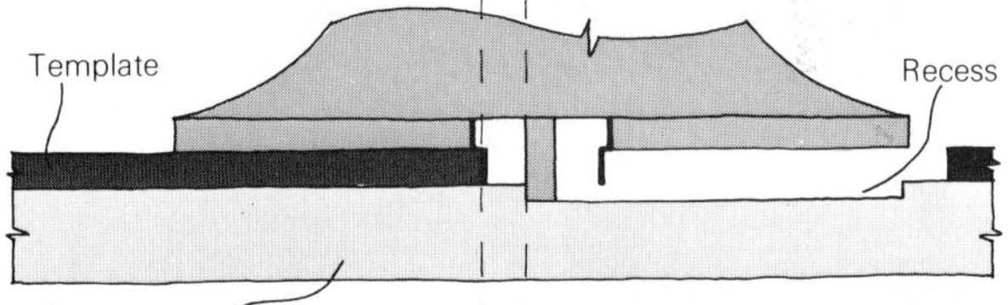

Template   Recess

Ground stock

3. Routing border

Change to ¾-in. guide and ⅛-in. bit, using same template. Note that groove spans edge between inlay and ground stock. Press border strip in with a hammer.

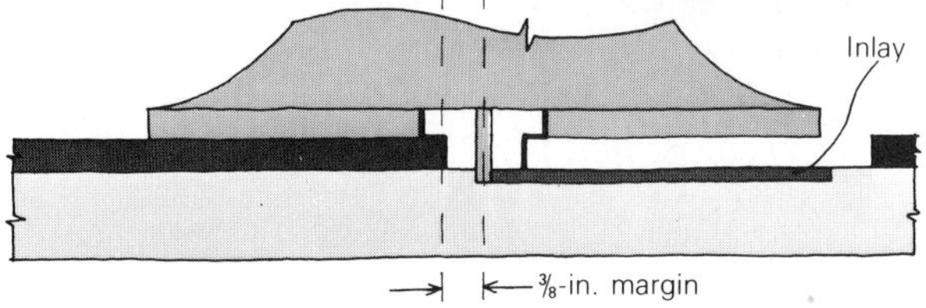

Inlay

³/₈-in. margin

A border of ¹/₁₆-in. or ⅛-in. holly, satinwood or black-dyed maple strips may be set in to frame the inlay. To do this, align the template over the inlay. Change to a ¾-in. guide and a ¹/₁₆-in. or ⅛-in. straight bit, depending upon the size of the strip to be inlaid, and adjust for the correct depth of cut. Move the router around the template with the guide held against the inside edge of the template. Clean out the groove, apply glue and press in the strip, carefully bending it to conform to the curve. Normally no clamping is necessary because the strip will hold well in the groove while the glue dries.

Template routing can also be used for setting in hinges, chest and wardrobe locks, and recessed draw pulls.   □

Eric Schramm designs and builds custom furniture in Los Gatos, Calif.

Improving the Fretsaw
Pivot guides handsawing of marquetry veneers

by Ed Kampe

In marquetry, it's difficult to use a fretsaw freehand with only a bird's-mouth jig for support. With a few years of practice, you might become accomplished with this contraption, but I've already used up my three score and ten, and the designer in me insisted that there must be a better method. I wanted a jig that could be clamped to a corner of the kitchen table, something for the shut-ins or for the person in a wheelchair. Marquetry is a wonderful hobby that combines art and craft. An easy-to-use fretsaw might help more people enjoy it.

With that in mind, I rigged up this jig, which is suitable for the double-bevel marquetry cutting method explained by Silas Kopf in "Marquetry on Furniture" on pp. 41-45. Instead of the entire tool moving up and down, my modified fretsaw is clamped to a wooden arm, which pivots on a carriage-bolt axle attached to the saw table. This setup has three advan-

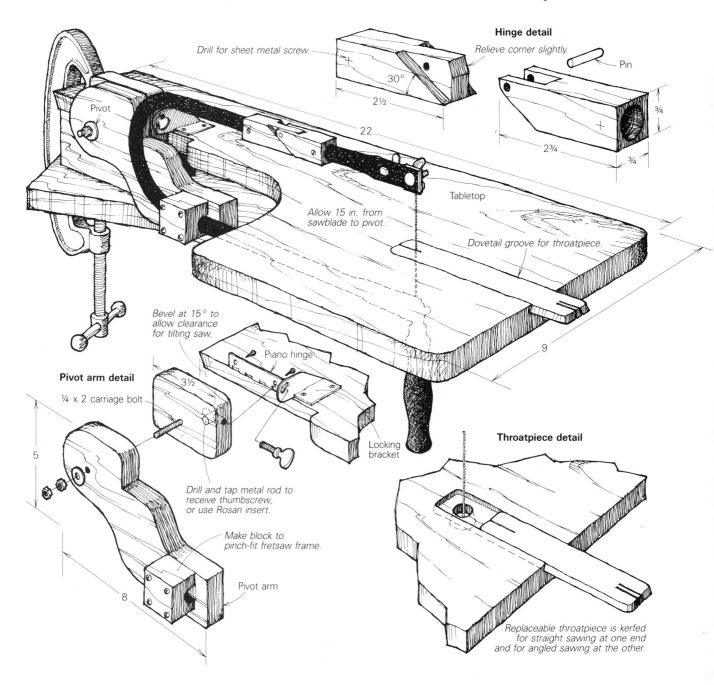

Drill for sheet metal screw.

Hinge detail

Relieve corner slightly.

Pin

30°

2½

2¾

¾

¾

Pivot

22

Tabletop

Allow 15 in. from sawblade to pivot.

Dovetail groove for throatpiece.

9

Bevel at 15° to allow clearance for tilting saw.

Piano hinge

Pivot arm detail

3½

¼ x 2 carriage bolt

5

Drill and tap metal rod to receive thumbscrew, or use Rosan insert.

Make block to pinch-fit fretsaw frame.

8

Pivot arm

Locking bracket

Throatpiece detail

Replaceable throatpiece is kerfed for straight sawing at one end and for angled sawing at the other.

Drawings: Jim Richey

tages. First, the saw is always held at the correct angle, freeing me from the task of sliding work and saw around in search of the narrow notch in the bird's-mouth. Second, the saw's hinged upper arm pivots out of the way when a blade must be threaded through the workpiece. And third, the veneer can be held stationary as the saw is stroked. This last feature is handy because when the blade reaches the bottom of its maximum stroke, it will have advanced about $\frac{5}{64}$ in., offering good control when cutting fragile or pointed parts.

As the drawing shows, I made my jig to about the dimensions of a small, power scroll saw. The table, saw bracket and tilting mechanism are of pine, but a good grade of $\frac{3}{4}$-in. plywood could be substituted. If unsupported, veneer will chip on the back side as it is cut. I solved this problem by inserting a throatpiece that slides in a 1-in. wide dovetailed groove milled in the tabletop. One end of the throatpiece is kerfed to accommodate the blade set at 90°; the other end has two kerfs at 12°, the angle I like for double-beveling.

The saw is clamped to a bracket, which is in turn attached to the table by a section of brass piano hinge. This allows the saw angle to be varied. A thumbscrew through a shopmade aluminum bracket locks the saw at the desired angle. I made my own barrel nut for the thumbscrew by drilling and tapping a $\frac{3}{8}$-in. steel rod. A wood screw, or better yet a thumbscrew threaded into a Rosan insert, would serve the same purpose. The best pivot point turned out to be 15 in. from the blade and just below the surface of the table.

If I had had access to a machine shop, I would have made the upper arm hinge from aluminum so that it could be smaller. As it was, I had to use wood, and maple seemed a good choice. So that you won't have to contend with clamping the odd-shaped pieces on the drill press, bore the blind holes for the saw frame before you shape the hinge parts. I didn't have the 0.515-in. ($\frac{33}{64}$-in.) bit to match the diameter of my saw frame, but an oversize $\frac{1}{2}$-in. masonry bit I found in my collection worked fine after I ground off a few thousandths of an inch. For accuracy, I drilled a $\frac{1}{2}$-in. hole first, and then, without changing the setup, enlarged it with my modified bit. Not all fretsaws have tubular frames (I got mine from Constantine's). If yours is of steel bar stock, you'll have to modify the mounting bracket and mortise the frame into the hinges.

I cut and shaped the hinge sections on my 4-in. Dremel saw. Doing it by hand is nearly as easy. With a backsaw, saw the angled cheeks and shoulders of the male section, then chisel the slot in the female part until you get a slip fit. For the hinge pin, I sacrificed a $\frac{5}{32}$-in. drill bit. Measuring the overall length of the hinge and subtracting the combined depth of the two holes tells you how long a section of the saw has to be cut out. Make sure that the blade clamps line up when you put the saw together. I fastened the hinge with sheet-metal screws driven through the wood and into the saw frame.

Installing a blade is easy. First, I clamp the jig to a comfortable work surface, which happens to be the desk in my den. I thread the blade through from the top and clamp it at the bottom. Resting the saw handle on my knee leaves both hands free to pivot the upper arm down and clamp the other end of the blade. □

Ed Kampe was a design engineer and general foreman in precision metalworking. He makes marquetry pictures in Zellwood, Fla.

Motor makes fretsawing fly

by Scott Littleton

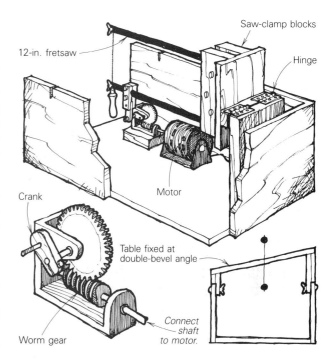

12-in. fretsaw

Saw-clamp blocks

Hinge

Crank

Motor

Table fixed at double-bevel angle

Connect shaft to motor.

Worm gear

As a marquetry beginner, I found that knife-cutting left my hands stiff and sore, so I set out to design and build a low-cost power scroll saw that would make a beveled cut. Ideally, a marquetry saw's blade should operate straight up and down. But a mechanism with a large throat to achieve this ideal seemed beyond my abilities. Some sketching showed me that a simple oscillating saw might work, since the force needed to cut veneer is small and the speed need not be great. One disadvantage of a rocking saw frame is that the cutting edge of the blade moves forward and back during the stroke. I found that with a short stroke ($\frac{3}{4}$ in.), the front-to-back motion is negligible.

I built my saw the simplest way I could and just slapped it together quickly, thinking it was an experiment to be improved on later. It works so well that the only improvement I may ever make is to increase the throat depth.

To make the saw, I clamped a 12-in. fretsaw between two bolted blocks. The blocks are attached to a hinged post mounted on a $\frac{3}{4}$-in. plywood base. To remove any side play from the saw, put the hinges in a bind, or use a piano hinge. Up-and-down motion is achieved through a small electric motor, a small worm gearbox (or gearmotor) and a simple crank mechanism. After having tried several speeds, I find that about 300 strokes per minute is my preference. The motor to power the unit need not be large. I've found that even a $\frac{1}{120}$-HP gearmotor (Dayton 200-RPM shaded pole gearmotor, stock #2Z812, about $18.50 in 1983) will cut two thicknesses of oak veneer without noticeably slowing down. □

Scott Littleton lives in Salt Lake City, Utah.

From *Fine Woodworking* magazine (November 1983) 43:60-61

Inlaying Mother-of-Pearl
Watching one banjo maker cut and fit a delicate design

by John Lively

Though most often found as decoration on musical instruments, mother-of-pearl inlays traditionally have graced a diversity of articles—furniture large and small, gunstocks and knife handles, walking sticks and billiard cues. Mother-of-pearl and its more colorful cousin, abalone shell, are sold in small, thin pieces (the box below lists some suppliers), that are quite abrasive, hence hard on tools, and extremely brittle. You can't just saw it as though it were maple veneer. A highly developed craft practiced by the Chinese as early as the 14th century, mother-of-pearl inlay was very popular among the 18th-century *ébénistes*, and it distinguishes the work of such

20th-century inheritors of that tradition as Louis Süe and Andre Mare.

To learn how to cut and inlay mother-of-pearl, I visited Richard Newman at his shop in Rochester, N.Y. He demonstrated his technique by cutting a stylized Georgian dolphin in pearl, then inlaying it into a piece of scrap ebony. Here's how he did it. (Note that he uses the jeweler's saw upside down from the orthodox way.)

From his stash of mother-of-pearl chips, Newman selected one and pasted a paper cartoon of the sea beast on top of it. Next, he clamped his bird's mouth (a rectangular block with

Sources of supply for mother-of-pearl and abalone

Mother-of-pearl does not come from the oyster that produces seed pearls, but from various bivalve mollusks, some of which grow as large as 2 ft. in diameter. Most pearl shell is imported from the western Pacific; the cold waters of Australia produce the finest shells, less likely to be damaged by sea worms, barnacles or other parasites. Colors range from white and grey to pink and deep gold; gold pearl, from the lip of the shell, is the most expensive cut. Some pieces of pearl are preferred for their evenness of color; others are irridescent and highly figured, sometimes desig-

Arthur Sweeney is a professional stringed-instrument maker. He lives in Napa, Calif.

nated wavy or fiddleback after the wood figures they resemble.

Abalone is cut from the shell of a monovalve mollusk native to southern Californian and Mexican waters. It is generally more spectacular than pearl, with black fracture lines along twisting planes of bright colors that blend and shift under changing light. There is green abalone, which has become rare, and there is larger, less expensive red abalone. The central portion of the shell, where the muscle attaches, is called the heart and is most prized. It looks something like crinkled tinfoil, sparkling with green, blue and red.

Suppliers cut mother-of-pearl and abalone with a lapidary saw, attending to the figure and curvature of the shell. The

pieces are irregularly shaped, usually about 1 in. square (a 3-in. piece is considered large). Then they're ground to thicknesses ranging from 0.035 in. to 0.060 in. The thicker stock is best for curved surfaces, like fretboards, and for fine lines and sharp curves. Some suppliers grade their stock "select" (for exceptional figure and size), "#1" (good and clear), and "#2" (some parasite damage). Cost is figured by the ounce, $15 to $25 an ounce being typical (1981). Some suppliers, as indicated below, will custom-cut designs; some provide pre-cut blanks in a limited number of designs.   —*Arthur Sweeney*

Suppliers:

Erika, 12731 Loma Rica Dr., Suite G, Grass Valley, Calif. 95945. Mother-of-pearl and abalone blanks.

Handy Trading Co., 8560 Venice Blvd., Los Angeles, Calif. 90034. Mother-of-pearl and abalone in bulk.

Pearl Works, Larry Sifel, Rt. 3, Box 98B, Mechanicsville, Md. 20659. Mother-of-pearl and abalone blanks; precut designs; will custom-cut designs.

Vitali Imports, 5944 Atlantic Boulevard, Maywood, Calif. 90270. Mother-of-pearl blanks.

David Russell Young, 7134 Balboa Boulevard, Van Nuys, Calif. 91406. Mother-of-pearl and abalone blanks.

Zaharoff Industries, 26 Max Ave., Hicksville, N.Y. 11801. Mother-of-pearl and abalone blanks; will custom-cut designs.   ☐

Chinese k'ang (a type of bed) from the Ming dynasty (1368-1644) exemplifies the sophistication of mother-of-pearl inlay work before it became popular in Europe. Metropolitan Museum of Art, gift of Mrs. Jean Mayzē, 1961.

From *Fine Woodworking* magazine (March 1981) 27:50-52

Very fragile and brittle, pearl must be sawn with a studied technique and special care. Left, with jeweler's saw and bird's mouth (the V-notched board clamped to his bench), Newman cuts a mythical sea beast from a mother-of-pearl chip. Top right, Dremel equipped with a tiny end mill routs the recess for the pearl inlay. It must fit easily, but with no gaps. Center, Newman uses an engraver's block to hold the stock when incising detail into the pearl. Engraver's blocks are necessary for good results, since engraving requires moving the work into the tool rather than the other way around, as is the case with carving wood. Engraved gouges filled with epoxy/aniline dye mixture delineate details and add depth to the finished dolphin (about twice actual size), right. Newman used black dye, but other colors would work as well.

a V-notch cut in one end) to his bench. With jeweler's saw in hand, handle up, teeth down, he proceeded to cut around the shape of the beast, using a #3 jeweler's blade (photo, above left). Sometimes moving the pearl into the blade and sometimes moving the blade into the pearl, his easy sawing rhythm kept the blade from binding, which, had it occurred, would have fractured the pearl. Rhythm, he told me, is especially important when sawing tight curves, because interrupting the up-and-down motion can snag the blade, chip the pearl and ruin the whole job.

While sawing away, Newman pointed out that pearl dust is toxic and said you should blow the dust away from your face. He uses a respirator when sawing it for extended periods, and warns that lung damage can result from inhaling too much of the powder. To saw the sharp points on the tail and pectoral fins, he always cut from the outside in, sawing out little loops in the waste part of the pearl to make space for a new angle of attack. This part of the job was slow-going, but the tedium paid off. The finished dolphin required only a few deft touches with a needle file to make its profile precisely right.

To prepare the ebony for inletting, he glued the pearl dolphin on the surface with Duco quick-dry cement. Then,

carefully, he traced around the figure with a sharp machinist's scribe, deepening the scratch a little at a time until the outline was clearly visible. Tracing complete, he slid a razor blade under the pearl and popped it free, leaving its silhouette behind. For routing out the area for inletting, Newman used a 2-flute, single-end micro-miniature end mill with a ⅛-in. shank (available from the Woodson Tool Co., 544 W. 132nd St., Gardena, Calif. 90248). The bit was mounted in a Dremel Moto-Tool equipped with a router base (photo, top right). Newman set the depth of cut slightly shallower than the thickness of the pearl. This end mill will cut a channel as narrow as 1/32 in., thus minimizing the areas that will need to be filled in later at sharp corners.

It took a little trial fitting and re-routing to make the pearl drop neatly into place. Next, Newman applied silver leaf to the back of the inlay, and then he mixed a pinch of ebony sanding dust into a batch of five-minute epoxy (full-cure epoxy is better), smeared some into the recess and inserted the dolphin, pushing down gently and letting the epoxy/dust mixture ooze out slowly. He covered the inlay with plastic wrap and clamped a block on top of it. After 30 minutes drying (the epoxy has to set hard), he removed the block and

Newman saws mother-of-pearl the traditional way.

filed, scraped and sanded the whole business flush with the surface of the wood. Whatever gaps there were between the pearl and the wood (I saw only a speck or two) had been neatly filled with the dust/epoxy mixture.

Sanding, of course, made powder of the original cartoon. But he had lots of them on hand (they're photocopies of his original drawing) and got another out to use as a guide for penciling on the blank form all of its details—eye, scales and frilly gill. To engrave these little details into the beast's surface, Newman secured the wood in an engraver's block (photo, previous page, center). Unlike carving wood, where one moves the tool into the work, engraving calls for moving the work into the tool, which is held almost stationary. The engraver's block, with its heavy hemispherical base, is designed for this. You can order one from Brownell's Inc., Rt. 2, Box 1, Montezuma, Iowa 50171, or from Paul H. Gesswein Co., 235 Park Ave. South, New York, N.Y. 10003. With a square high-speed steel graver, Newman incised the details into the pearl. You can engrave pearl without an engraver's block, but it's not easy. You'll have to clamp and re-clamp the stock to your bench because you will need both hands to control the tool, and your avenues of approaching the work will be limited, since you must lock your arms to your sides and move your whole body into the cut.

With the engraving done, Newman made another epoxy puddle, mixed in powdered black aniline dye and spread the inky stuff over the entire surface of the pearl, filling in the engraved areas. When the mess had dried, he sanded it down flush with the surface of the wood. Upon lifting the sanding block and wiping the dust away, some three hours after taking saw in hand, there lay the finished dolphin, its incised features boldly alive and vividly defined.　□

Inlaid lap desk

This lap desk took Larry Robinson of Petaluma, Calif., 100 hours to make. It's of crotch and curly maple, bordered by ebony and inlaid with some 400 pieces of various woods, metals, and other materials, including crushed blue glass, crazy-lace agate, ivory, mother-of-pearl, abalone and opal. Robinson says he uses cyanoacrylate (Crazy) glue because it adheres to anything and it dries clear and free of the bubbles that characterize many epoxy mixes. He prefers to work with relatively thick materials (⅛-in. wood and 18-ga. to 20-ga. metals) because they're easier to saw and less likely to sand through than thinner stock. After sawing with a 4/0 or a 6/0 jeweler's blade, he tack-glues the pieces to the surface to be inlaid and scribes, then highlights the outline with chalk dust before routing. Combining various materials requires that the least dense ones be thickest and that all the pieces sit flush on the bottom of the inlay cavity, so sanding can bring their top surfaces flush.

Photo: Dave Murphy

A Jigsaw for Cutting Delicate Stock
Treadle power and spring return are ideal for pearl inlay

by Ken Parker

Cutting mother-of-pearl and abalone is difficult at best. The material is abrasive, very hard, brittle and rife with natural faults. As I stubbornly tried to saw out my signature, it became apparent that I didn't have the right tool.

Usually, pearl is sawn by hand with a jeweler's saw, against a bird's mouth (see p. 79). Any skewing of the fragile blade may snap the pearl. Furthermore, a small piece is hard to hold flat with one hand against the lifting force of the return stroke. As you struggle to control the cut, hold the work and keep the stroke perpendicular, tension builds quickly and it's easy to apply forces that exceed the material's strength.

Sawing pearl in a power jigsaw presents different problems. Typically the slowest speed is much too fast and the stroke too short; instead of cutting efficiently, the sawteeth slide against the pearl, overheating and dulling quickly. Lubricating with light oils or beeswax to keep cutting temperatures lower and to ease the work obscures the cut with pearl-dust sludge and loosens the glue holding the paper pattern.

Industry uses small, template-controlled overhead pin routers to produce elaborate inlays in guitars, banjos and other stringed instruments. The single-flute, solid-carbide cutters are air/mist cooled and spin as fast as 100,000 RPM. But besides the prohibitive cost of such machines for the individual craftsman, these routers are still unable to make the finest cuts. A 4/0 jeweler's saw, for example, takes a 0.008-in. kerf, while router bits are usually 0.022 in. in diameter. Thus hand-cut pearl can have sharp inside corners that machine-cut pearl can't.

My solution is the foot-operated saw shown here. It is simple to build and has some important advantages for cutting pearl. It can be used as well for cutting veneer, especially for marquetry, though you would probably want to add a flywheel and rocker treadle for momentum. (You can adapt the design of the old Singer sewing machine, or you can build one from scratch.) Foot power in my pearl-cutting saw is direct, and the return stroke is by way of a spring. The blade can thus be stopped instantly to prevent a strained piece from breaking. I clamp the upper part of the saw in my bench vise with the table at chin height. This provides good visibility and a relaxed posture; note that the teeth face the operator and the saw frame is behind the work. I rest my elbows on the bench and my chin on the table, blowing dust away with every stroke. There are two hands free to hold and maneuver the work, and the small table allows me to grip tightly, fingers on top and thumbs underneath.

Before describing the construction of the saw, some general remarks on cutting pearl: Use the largest blade possible for the contour you have to cut, and replace the blade before it gets dull, saving it for less critical work. As with all saw or file cuts in hard or tenacious material, the tool must move slowly enough to take a maximum cut per tooth. Excessive speed produces friction and dulls the saw while cutting very little, as the teeth do not fully engage the work. Feel each tooth dig in and cut and the job will go surprisingly quickly.

It's best after pasting your paper pattern on the pearl (I use mucilage) to drill a hole at one end of the design and work from there instead of sawing in from the edge of the pearl. This provides support around the design. Try to cut exactly outside the pattern line. The only filing necessary should be on inside corners and at the ends of cuts. Jeweler's sawblades begin and end with graduated teeth. By using the top ¼-in. of the blade when turning tight corners, the "broaching" action aggressively chops out the waste and gives the blade room to turn. Furthermore, the extra rigidity at the blade end aids in accurate turning.

Construction—Begin with a rigid saw-frame. It is essential that there be no side play because racking strain can shatter

Foot-powered jigsaw designed especially for cutting delicate mother-of-pearl and abalone is mounted in the bench vise. A drawing of Parker's jigsaw appears on the following page.

From *Fine Woodworking* magazine (March 1981) 27:53-55

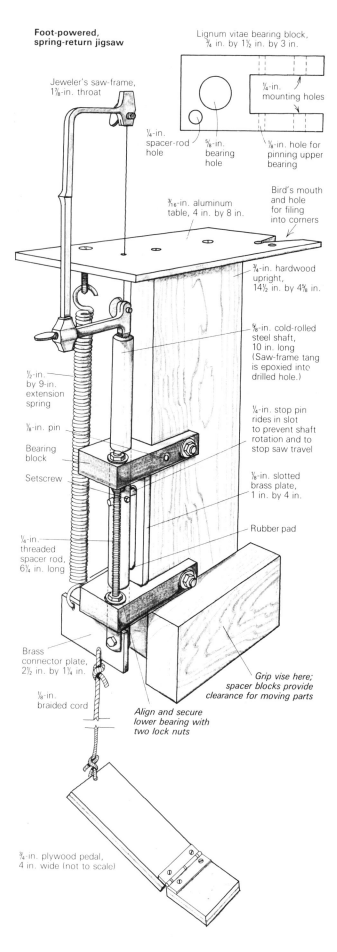

Foot-powered, spring-return jigsaw

Lignum vitae bearing block, ¾ in. by 1½ in. by 3 in.

Jeweler's saw-frame, 1⅞-in. throat

¼-in. mounting holes

¼-in. spacer-rod hole

⅝-in. bearing hole

⅛-in. hole for pinning upper bearing

Bird's mouth and hole for filing into corners

³⁄₁₆-in. aluminum table, 4 in. by 8 in.

¾-in. hardwood upright, 14½ in. by 4⅝ in.

⅝-in. cold-rolled steel shaft, 10 in. long (Saw-frame tang is epoxied into drilled hole.)

½-in. by 9-in. extension spring

⅛-in. pin

Bearing block

Setscrew

¼-in. stop pin rides in slot to prevent shaft rotation and to stop saw travel

⅛-in. slotted brass plate, 1 in. by 4 in.

Rubber pad

¼-in. threaded spacer rod, 6¼ in. long

Brass connector plate, 2½ in. by 1¼ in.

⅛-in. braided cord

Align and secure lower bearing with two lock nuts

Grip vise here; spacer blocks provide clearance for moving parts

¾-in. plywood pedal, 4 in. wide (not to scale)

the fragile pearl. The best style of saw-frame has a square shaft for a back member; its blade is tensioned by a thumbscrew. I used a jeweler's saw-frame with a 1⅞-in. throat, which can be had from a jeweler's supply house, as can an assortment of blades.

The tang of the saw-frame is mounted in a ⅝-in. cold-rolled steel shaft (more on that later) and the shaft slides up and down in a pair of bearings attached to a hardwood upright. Lignum vitae works beautifully for these low-speed bearings. It is easily sawn and drilled, it is hard and resistant to abrasion, and it is naturally oily, though I keep the bearings moist with mineral oil when the saw is in use. Saw the outside dimensions carefully to minimize the need to true up the lignum by hand; it will dull all but the toughest edge tools. Seal freshly cut surfaces immediately with tung oil or wax to prevent checking that will ruin the part.

Spade bits are convenient for drilling the ⅝-in. bearing hole because they can be filed to size. Test-drill in a scrap of lignum, coat the inside of the hole with mineral oil and see if you still have enough clearance. The oil will cause the wood to swell and make the hole minutely smaller. To get a clean cut, clamp the work and use high speed and slow feed. Once you have a good fit in a test block, prepare the two bearing blocks for drilling by stacking and gluing them together with a dab of 5-minute (weak) epoxy or paper and white glue between; assembly and alignment will go smoothly if the blocks have been squared, drilled and slotted precisely. Drill the ⅝-in. and ¼-in. vertical holes and saw the slots. Cross-holes for the mounting bolts may also be conveniently drilled before the blocks are split apart. Do not drill the ⅛-in. hole in the upper block at this time; it's more precise to drill and pin the block after it's mounted on the upright. Be sure to witness-mark the blocks to preserve alignment.

For the upright, use a piece of stable, straight-grained hardwood. Warping here can impede the saw's action. Thickness the stock, and square the edges and ends accurately. Spacer blocks are added later, as shown in the drawing, to provide clearance for moving parts when the saw is gripped in the bench vise.

This is the end of the woodworking part of this project. If you have never worked with metal before, you will benefit from the following primer. You'll be surprised to discover how nicely some of your woodworking tools will handle metal.
Sawing—At least two teeth in the work, as usual.
—*Steel*: Hacksaw; use heavy cutting oil; slow, even strokes.
—*Aluminum*: Bandsaws beautifully with standard woodcutting blades; light cutting oil or kerosene may be used for heavier cuts; wipe tires dry after cutting.
—*Brass*: Bandsaws well; use dull blade; do not lubricate.
Drilling—Smaller holes, higher speeds, lighter feeds. Use twist drills; center-punch the hole location; clamp the work or hold it in a vise.
—*Steel*: low speeds; heavy feed; lubricate with oil. For easy cutting and accurate hole size, drill with a succession of drills of increasing diameter; for example, for a ¼-in. hole, drill first with a ³⁄₃₂-in. drill, then a ³⁄₁₆-in., then a ¼-in.
—*Aluminum*: Fairly high speeds; light feed; lubricate with light oil or kerosene.
—*Brass*: Medium speeds; medium feed; do not lubricate. Best results come from honing the rake angle to 0°, thus preventing the drill from grabbing or screwing into the work.

To mount the saw-frame in the ⅝-in. cold-rolled steel shaft,

Drawing: Ric Lopez

Parker's design allows a comfortable working posture, sensitive control of the stroke and a good view of the work. Thin, narrow sawtable, left, allows work to be held down securely between fingers and thumbs. Center, Parker cuts the mortise for his mother-of-pearl signature (0.030 in. wide) using a Foredom mounted in a simple, adjustable-leg tripod.

first remove the saw-frame handle and determine the diameter and depth of the hole that will accommodate the tang. If in doubt, drill oversize because the tang will be fixed with epoxy, which will fill any voids. Cross-drill the shaft for the stop pin that will slide in the brass track on the upright's back edge. The stop pin may be retained by a setscrew epoxied in place or, if a bolt is used, locked in place with nuts. Notch the bottom end of the steel shaft using a hacksaw, and file the notch to fit a brass or aluminum plate. The plate, bolted in place, serves to transmit the drive and spring-return forces to the shaft.

Now make the brass track, which keeps the shaft from rotating, limits travel and houses rubber pads for absorbing shock at the ends of travel. You can mill the track from solid stock or construct it from strips. Alternately, you can rout the slot in the edge of the upright, although a separate brass plate allows you to set up the saw with a blade and determine where the stops should be. Travel will be the slot length minus the stop-pin diameter and the thickness of the rubber pads. Travel on my saw is just under 3 in., the length of toothed area on a 5-in. jeweler's sawblade.

I made my table out of ³⁄₁₆-in. aluminum plate. You can vary the size to suit the work; a thin, narrow table is good for cutting inlay because you can fit your thumbs and fingers around to pinch the work to the table (photo, above left), decreasing the likelihood that it will lift and break on the return stroke. Drill holes in the table for mounting, for passing the blade through (this should be as small as possible) and for attaching the spring. Also drill a couple of holes or cut a bird's mouth to be used for filing at the end of the table opposite the blade.

Assembly—Hold the saw sideways during assembly. Mark positions for the bearing blocks, and clamp them to the up-

right, shimming the throat of the blocks out with thin cardboard so that as the bearings wear they can be angled to take up slop. Get the shaft to move smoothly and drill through the upright for the mounting bolts. Insert bolts, washers and nuts; tighten and make sure the shaft is still free. Drill the ⅛-in. hole through the upper bearing, pin it in place and remove the cardboard shims. Slide the threaded spacer rod, with washers and nuts, through the bearings, and lock it in place in the upper bearing. Adjust the lower nuts to bring the lower bearing into line, confirmed by easy movement of the shaft. Position the brass track on the edge of the upright and test the stroke to be sure the top teeth can be brought into the work. The track may be screwed, pinned or epoxied in place. Insert the stop pin in the shaft, and see that the shaft runs freely without rotation.

To mount the saw-frame in proper alignment on the shaft, install a blade on center in the saw-frame clamps, fill the hole in the top of the shaft with epoxy and slip the saw-frame tang in. Slide the shaft up and down and observe the blade travel using a try square on the table. Align the saw-frame accordingly and hold or support it in place while the epoxy hardens. If you need to reset the tang, heat the shaft end with a torch; most epoxies give up before 300°F.

Position the table so the blade passes through and mark and drill for shankless wood screws in the end grain of the upright. Screw the table into place, making sure it is perfectly square with the blade.

Bolt the connecting plate in place at the bottom of the shaft and attach the spring from it to the table. The cord from the pedal also attaches to the plate. With the heel of the pedal screwed to the floor and the upright clamped in your bench end-vise, you're ready to saw. □

Ken Parker makes arch-top guitars in New York City.

Laying Plastic Laminates

Understanding the basics of this ubiquitous "veneer"

by Jack Gavin

Let me say, before any purists dash off angry letters to the editor, that I don't consider plastic laminates to be fine woodwork. As a custom cabinetmaker, however, I've laid miles of the stuff, and for every solid cherry secretary or walnut armoire I do, I am offered ten Formica kitchens. So knowledge of the skills has become an economic necessity. Also, a lot of furnituremakers are discovering that new laminate products and techniques add a colorful dimension to their work.

Plastic laminates had their beginning at the turn of the century when Dr. Leo Bakeland, a Belgian scientist, invented Bakelite, the first plastic. Bakeland offered his invention to the Westinghouse Company as an electrical insulator, but Westinghouse wasn't interested. A young Westinghouse chemist named Dan O'Connor, however, impregnated paper and cloth with Bakeland's resin and formed his own company in Cincinnati, Ohio. He called the new product and the company Formica: "for mica," since mica was the premium insulator of the day.

Formica was originally used for such diverse products as radio vacuum-tube bases and gears for the Model-T Ford. In the late 1930s, the idea of laminating a thin surface of this abrasion-resistant plastic to counters and tabletops was tried. After World War II, the idea caught on and grew into a multi-million dollar industry.

Plastic laminates are made of six or less layers of kraft paper (depending on the thickness) that are impregnated with phenolic resin (Bakelite), and then covered with a sheet of colored or patterned paper and sealed with a layer of melamine plastic. Although "Formica" has become the generic name for decorative plastic laminates, there are a number of other laminate manufacturers besides the Formica Corp. Nevamar, Wilsonart, Lamin-Art, and Melamite are some of the many different brands, each a quality product. I've seen 30-year-old countertops that were beginning to wear through, showing a brown tone from the kraft paper beneath, but you can expect an even longer life than that from the modern surfaces, provided that they are well cemented to the proper core material (see box, p. 86).

Laminates come imprinted with simulated wood grain, simulated stone, stripes, grids, raised designs and a seemingly infinite variety of colors. Prices range from $.60 to about $3.50 per sq. ft. (1984 prices), depending on brand and design. Each company has color charts and makes boxes of samples of their different varieties, and a supplier will be happy to give you one of these for the brand he carries. Plastic laminates are usually stocked in widths up to 5 ft. and in lengths up to 12 ft. Instead of asking your supplier what he's got, tell him what size you need and he'll probably have something close to it, or he can order it for you. You also have a choice of two thicknesses, 1/16-in. and 1/32-in., called horizontal and vertical grade, respectively. Use horizontal grade whenever possible—particularly on surfaces subject to abrasion. Vertical grade is cheaper, and is good for curved surfaces, but it will show core irregularities on flat surfaces. Some laminates come with a plastic film over the surface. Leave it on until the job is done—it's there to protect the surface from your tools.

Visually check each sheet for damage. Unlike wood, scratched plastic laminate cannot be fixed. The sheets can be transported flat in a truck, or rolled and tied. If you roll a sheet, make sure you tape the inside edge to prevent the laminate from scratching itself as it is unrolled.

Seams where edges join can be filled with a product called Seamfil, available from laminate suppliers. It's a lacquer-

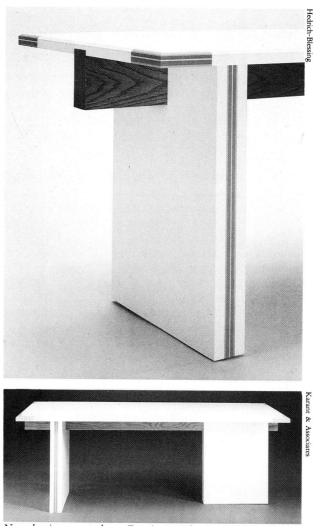

New laminates, such as Formica's ColorCore, offer decoration beyond the usual wood-surface treatments. This table, designed by Milton Glaser, is detailed with ColorCore epoxied into a multicolored sandwich and then sliced into thin ribbons.

based compound that dries very quickly. It comes with color charts that tell how to mix an exact match to whatever color plastic laminate you buy. A filled seam never looks as good as a single piece, however, and Seamfil won't fix scratches.

Cement—The standard glue for plastic laminates is contact cement, and several types are sold by stores that sell laminates. Contact cements have a bad reputation for gluing wood to wood, but when one of the materials is stable and nonporous, as plastic laminate is, contact cement forms a permanent bond. These cements are neoprene rubber dissolved in various solvents. Spread on both surfaces and allowed to dry, the rubber coatings stick to each other when the sheets are pressed together. For all-around use, I recommend the regular industrial grade.

A word of warning here. Industrial contact cement is *extremely* flammable, so much so that if the vapors are allowed to collect in a small room, something as insignificant as a cigarette or a pilot light can ignite them explosively. Work in a well-ventilated area, and even so, *always* wear an organic-vapor mask. The solvents in industrial contact cement are the same as in airplane glue, and we all know the effects of sniffing that. Some suppliers may refuse to sell industrial cements to amateurs, or may carry them only in commercial-size 5-gal. pails. If that's the case (it may even be the law in your area), then use whatever cement you can get. In any event, heed the label, both for safety warnings and for application instructions. Hardware-store cement is less explosive than industrial cement, and there's a nonflammable latex-based contact cement, too, but it takes significantly longer to dry. Otherwise, all types are worked the same way.

One type of cement is specially formulated for use in spray guns, but spraying isn't practical except for large production shops—you can spend up to $3,000 just for the gear.

Cutting laminates—I cut most of my plastic laminate on a tablesaw, using a triple-chip blade. So the material won't slip under the fence, I tape a strip of ¼-in. plywood or hardboard to the table next to the fence and run the laminate over it. The laminate sheets must be cut slightly larger than the piece they'll be laid upon, say, ⅛ in. oversize all around. They'll be trimmed flush after application.

The tablesaw gives the quickest and most precise cut, but a plastic scribe or tinsnips work, too. To cut with a scribe, mark the face side and score repeatedly, then crack with the score-line over a table edge. The break will run diagonally through the thickness of the sheet, so leave the sheet about ⅜ in. to ½ in. oversize in all directions. Tinsnips leave small cracks perpendicular to the cut, requiring a ½-in. allowance.

Order of events—We'll go into detail as things come up, but here's the general plan for, say, a countertop. First, trim the core to its final size. Then cut a big piece of plastic laminate for the top surface and narrow strips for all the core edges you plan to laminate. Remember to cut the laminate slightly oversize. Next, apply cement to both of the core's long edges and to the laminate strips that will cover them, taking care to keep cement off adjacent surfaces and edges. Laminate the long edges and trim the surplus flush. Follow the same procedure for the short edges. Finally, cement the top piece and trim it flush. If the job calls for a splashboard, laminate it as a separate piece and attach it later. For structural pieces such as

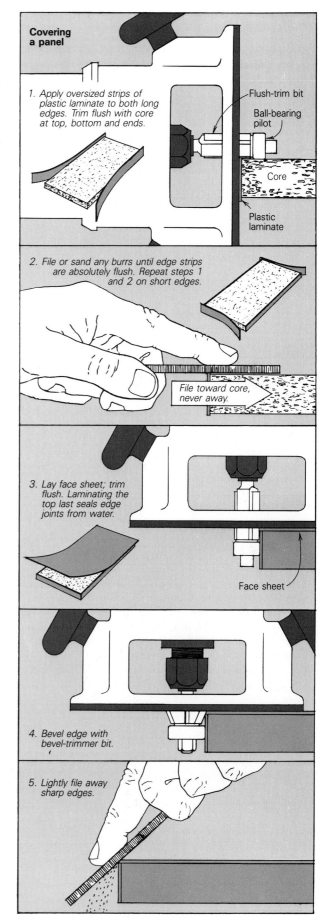

Covering a panel

1. Apply oversized strips of plastic laminate to both long edges. Trim flush with core at top, bottom and ends.

Flush-trim bit
Ball-bearing pilot
Core
Plastic laminate

2. File or sand any burrs until edge strips are absolutely flush. Repeat steps 1 and 2 on short edges.

File toward core, never away.

3. Lay face sheet; trim flush. Laminating the top last seals edge joints from water.

Face sheet

4. Bevel edge with bevel-trimmer bit.

5. Lightly file away sharp edges.

Tricks, tips, cores and new products

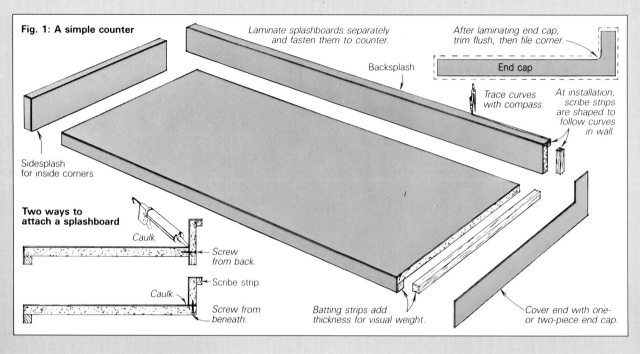

Fig. 1: A simple counter

Laminate splashboards separately and fasten them to counter.

After laminating end cap, trim flush, then file corner.

End cap

Backsplash

Trace curves with compass.

At installation, scribe strips are shaped to follow curves in wall.

Sidesplash for inside corners

Two ways to attach a splashboard

Caulk.

Screw from back.

Scribe strip

Caulk.

Screw from beneath.

Batting strips add thickness for visual weight.

Cover end with one- or two-piece end cap.

You can lay plastic laminate on almost any stable core. Solid wood, of course, moves too much, so you'll want man-made materials. For cabinet doors and drawer faces, I prefer medium-density fiberboard because it doesn't warp. Thickness can be either ⅝ in. or ¾ in. A ¾-in. door with ¹⁄₁₆-in. laminate on both sides turns out ⅞ in. thick, which may look a little clunky. For the cabinets themselves, I often use hardwood plywood, because it holds hinge screws better, but I wouldn't use it for any unsupported surfaces.

Countertops can be either ¾-in. plywood or fiberboard. There's a tradeoff—fiberboard is my first choice, because it's suitably "dead" (you don't want a counter to be resonant or springy), but it's heavy. If I'm going to have to carry a 12-ft. countertop up three flights of stairs, you can bet it'll be plywood instead. Whichever material you use, screw or glue a batting strip to the edge of your counter so that the finished edge will be 1 in. to 1½ in. thick (figure 1).

Edges can be covered with laminate or decorated with wood trim milled to any shape that suits your fancy, as in figure 2. Plastic or rubber T-molding, slipped into a kerf cut in the panel's edge, is also a good edge treatment. One source of T-molding is Outwater Plastics, 99 President St., Passaic, N.J. 07055.

I've never had any luck trying to lay new laminate over old. On one job a while ago, we tried to cover a curved surface with laminate, then cover that with another sheet of laminate that was

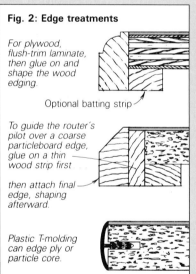

Fig. 2: Edge treatments

For plywood, flush-trim laminate, then glue on and shape the wood edging.

Optional batting strip

To guide the router's pilot over a coarse particleboard edge, glue on a thin wood strip first

then attach final edge, shaping afterward.

Plastic T-molding can edge ply or particle core.

itself covered with rift-maple veneer. *Everything* delaminated. We did the whole job over, using epoxy.

Laminates make fine wall coverings, too—have you ever taken a good look at the inside of an elevator? You can bond sheets directly to sheetrock, but I generally cover both sides of ½-in. particleboard and hang these panels on Z-clips (special hardware that allows the panels to be lifted off the walls when necessary).

ColorCore is a new (albeit expensive) Formica Corp. product that's the same color all the way through. Hence there's no dark line at the joints, and a careful workman can make an apparently seamless job. But ColorCore is less forgiving

of joint irregularities, and may show contact-cement lines, too. White glue is the recommended adhesive, because it dries clear, but you have to clamp down the laminate until the glue cures. With a sharp bit, you can rout shallow decorative patterns into the surface, and, by laying different colors atop each other, bevel panel edges into multicolored stripe designs. Laminate suppliers also have a variety of other new "designer" products. At the rate things are developing, your shop could end up first-on-the-block without half trying.

Many types of plastic laminates can be heated and cemented around narrow curves, forming a permanent bend upon cooling. Such "postformed" work has been around a long time. Everybody has seen single-sheet countertops that begin with a rolled front edge which sweeps across the counter and up the splashboard. Most postforming is done in factories, but the technique is feasible for a small shop and limited production, too. The Formica Corp. will send a detailed bulletin on the process if you ask—the low-end investment in equipment is less than $400 (1984 prices).

The Formica Corp.'s Information Center (114 Mayfield Ave., Edison, N.J. 08837) distributes numerous other technical bulletins, including a how-to guide. If you outline your project to them in a letter, they'll send relevant bulletins and color charts. Formica's technical specialist, Walter T. Davis, will give advice about tricky jobs over the phone at (513) 786-3048. —*J.G.*

countertops, you don't have to laminate both sides, but other parts, such as doors, require it or they will warp.

Spreading cement—Apply contact cement with a brush, a roller or a glue-spreader, spreading it as thinly as possible. Globs dry slowly and will cause a bump when the laminate is laid down. Take care to keep the area clean, because sawdust or chips that get caught in the glue will ruin the bond and are maddening to remove. The surface of the cement should dry evenly glossy. Edges of plywood, particleboard or fiberboard should have at least three coats, each applied after the previous coat has dried. Even on faces, it's a good idea to put a second coat in a 2-in. band around the perimeter.

For applying cement to narrow or tight areas, use a small brush with natural bristles (nylon will dissolve). It costs less to throw cheap brushes away than to buy enough solvent to clean decent ones. If you are edging a few similarly sized pieces, you can stack them and apply glue to the whole stack at once, which helps keep the faces free of cement. I've used a natural-bristle scrub brush for large areas such as countertops, but they are more easily done with a roller. Regular paint rollers will dissolve, but "high-solvent" roller sleeves, designed for spreading epoxy resins, work well. These are available wherever plastic laminates are sold. I prefer a roller with a short nap, rather than a knobby one. If you want a small roller for edges and tight spots, you can bandsaw the regular length into smaller pieces.

The cement should dry in 15 to 30 minutes, and remain ready-to-stick for a couple of hours. Don't wait too long, though, because the cement gradually loses its adhesiveness. The spread cement is ready when it is dry to the touch and has returned to room temperature. If the surface feels cool, it is still losing solvents and should be allowed to dry further.

Applying the laminate—Once the contact-cemented surfaces touch each other, they will stick, so you must be very careful to align the pieces before contact. This is relatively easy with edges and small pieces, but with larger panels it is best to lay out thin sticks—venetian-blind slats, dowels or something similar—about 12 in. apart on top of the panel, and then lay the laminate on top of them. Make sure these sticks are clean and splinter-free, because anything that gets caught underneath the laminate will cause a bump in the surface. Once the laminate has been centered over the panel, remove the sticks one at a time, consecutively, and press the laminate down. Work from one end, so as not to trap air bubbles, and progress down the length of the counter. When all the sticks are out (be sure to get them all), press the laminate down with a rubber mallet, a padded block and a hammer, or a hard roller called a J-roller—suppliers sell them.

Personally, I don't use sticks anymore. With the help of an assistant, I align one long edge and let the panel drop, an action similar to closing a book. It's a neat trick, but it requires some skill, so I wouldn't suggest it for beginners.

When making a lot of interior partitions, or a set of colored drawer bottoms, you can save a lot of trimming time by laminating an entire sheet of plastic laminate to the core material first, then tablesawing the pieces to size. To eliminate chipping while cutting, laminate only one side and run the panel through the tablesaw face-up. Then cover the other side of each piece and trim as usual. If you want to put laminate on the inside of a cabinet, be sure to do it before you assemble the cabinet. This will save you many, many hours of grief.

Moisture may cause delamination. Plan edges and joints so that water will run off, rather than into the seam. When installing a sink, most good workmen take pains to seal the core by applying a strip of laminate around the edges of the hole, in addition to caulking the rim of the sink.

Once applied, laminates can be removed, though the procedure is messy and time-consuming. Lift an edge slightly with a chisel and apply solvent. You can gradually remove the laminate without breaking it. Methyl ethyl ketone (known as MEK and sold in paint stores) will dissolve flammable cements, but it is flammable itself and it won't soften nonflammable cements; 1-1-1 trichloroethane works on both kinds of cement, and won't burn. But wear your vapor mask and gloves in any case, as both solvents are nasty. When dry, the laminate and panel can be reglued and reattached.

Trimming—Once the laminate has adhered, it must be trimmed flush with the core. The best tool is a router with a flush-trim bit, that is, a ½-in. straight carbide bit with a ball-bearing pilot on the end. This allows you to use the core itself as a guide. Don't try a bit with a steel pilot—it's guaranteed to burn the plastic surface. If you plan a lot of laminating, it's worth having a small, one-handed router called a laminate trimmer. The ease of use it affords is well worth its $100 price tag (1984). When using a router, wear goggles or a face shield to protect your eyes from laminate chips.

To trim an edge, hold the router horizontal and guide the pilot bearing along the face of the core, keeping the router's base square against the edge. The objective is to cut the edge strip exactly even with the face, so the face sheet will overlap it without gaps. Chances are, you'll need to do some filing, because flush-trim bits often cut slightly oversize, especially if they've been sharpened more than once. File toward the core to prevent chipping. I use a smooth file for narrow edges and, when I have the room, a belt sander. You can do the entire trimming job with these tools if you don't have a router.

When routing, it's important to keep the bearing free of plastic chips and cement. WD-40 will help dissolve any glue that binds in the bearing, and a few drops of light oil will keep it rolling. If a bearing clogs tight, try soaking it in solvent to restore it. A clogged bearing will burn a ¼-in. wide swath across whatever surface it is riding on, so a little preventive maintenance is a good idea. For extra insurance on really glossy surfaces, you can run a line of masking tape for the bearing to ride on. In a pinch, you can try to clean up a burned surface with 400-grit wet-or-dry sandpaper, but it will never look the same as before, even if you lacquer it to restore the shine. It's best to replace the piece.

When all the laminating is done, clean off excess glue with MEK or lacquer thinner. The edges should be square and sharp. To give the edges a finished look, use a bevel trimmer, which is similar to a flush-trim bit, but cuts a chamfer instead of a square edge. Bevel trimmers come in various angles: 15° and 22° are standard, and even 45° can be used. The greater the angle, the more the inner layer of the laminate will show on the top surface, sometimes desirable for contrast or to make the plastic laminate look thicker. In any case, a smooth file relieves sharp edges left by the router. □

Jack Gavin is a cabinetmaker and furnituremaker in New York City.

Index

FINE WOODWORKING
Editorial Staff, 1975-1986

Paul Bertorelli
Mary Blaylock
Dick Burrows
Jim Cummins
Katie de Koster
Ruth Dobsevage
Tage Frid
Roger Holmes
Cindy Howard
John Kelsey
Linda Kirk
Nancy-Lou Knapp
John Lively
Rick Mastelli
Nina Perry
Jim Richey
Paul Roman
David Sloan
Nancy Stabile
Laura Tringali
Linda D. Whipkey

FINE WOODWORKING
Art Staff, 1975-1986

Roger Barnes
Kathleen Creston
Deborah Fillion
Lee Hov
Betsy Levine
Lisa Long
E. Marino III
Karen Pease
Roland Wolf

FINE WOODWORKING
Production Staff, 1975-1986

Claudia Applegate
Barbara Bahr
Jennifer Bennett
Pat Byers
Mark Coleman
Deborah Cooper
Kathleen Davis
David DeFeo
Michelle Fryman
Mary Galpin
Dinah George
Barbara Hannah
Annette Hilty
Margot Knorr
Jenny Long
Johnette Luxeder
Gary Mancini
Laura Martin
Mary Eileen McCarthy
JoAnn Muir
Cynthia Lee Nyitray
Kathryn Olsen
Mary Ann Snieckus
Barbara Snyder